Thinking Out Loud

Thinking Out Loud

Love, Grief and
Being Mum and Dad

RIO FERDINAND

WITH DECCA AITKENHEAD

HODDER &
STOUGHTON

First published in Great Britain in 2017 by Hodder & Stoughton
An Hachette UK company

1

A CIP catalogue record for this title is available from the British Library

Hardback ISBN 978 1 473 67023 5
Trade Paperback ISBN 978 1 473 67024 2
eBook ISBN 978 1 473 67026 6

Typeset in Celeste by Palimpsest Book Production Ltd, Falkirk, Stirlingshire

Printed and bound by CPI Group (UK) Ltd, Croydon, CR0 4YY

Hodder & Stoughton policy is to use papers that are natural,
renewable and recyclable products and made from wood grown in sustainable
forests. The logging and manufacturing processes are expected to conform to the
environmental regulations of the country of origin.

Hodder & Stoughton Ltd
Carmelite House
50 Victoria Embankment
London EC4Y 0DZ

www.hodder.co.uk

*In loving memory of my wife Rebecca and mum Janice,
and to my children Lorenz, Tate and Tia.*

CONTENTS

IF YOU ARE anything like I used to be, this book might not look like your idea of a good read. I couldn't ever have seen myself reading a book like this until about a year ago. If anyone had told me I would actually write it, I would have called them crazy.

I became a professional footballer when I was fifteen. I'm thirty-eight now. A lot has happened since I first signed for West Ham, and I've changed in all kinds of ways – but one thing remains as true of me today as it was all those years ago. I have always, as anyone who knows me will tell you, been fanatically private.

All I ever wanted was to be a world-class footballer. Younger players seem to think of fame as the prize for success, but to me, it has only ever been the price. I wanted respect for my performance as a player; I didn't want attention off the pitch. *OK!* photo shoots and a celebrity wedding to a famous wife were not for me. It's no secret that Premier League football pays very well, these days, and I have been able to buy a lot of luxuries – but nothing is more precious to me than my privacy.

But on 1 May 2015 my world fell apart. My wife Rebecca died of breast cancer, leaving me to bring up our three children alone. I retired from professional football later that month, and for the first time in my life I didn't have a clue what I was doing. I didn't even know how to work the washing-machine. I had always been used to winning, but now I was out of my depth. All I knew was that my kids needed me, and if I was going to help them, I was going to have to ask for help too.

To say this was not easy would be putting it mildly. To be the best as a sportsman, you have to train your mind to think in a very particular way, and I learned to do so from a very young age. You cannot afford to feel ordinary human emotions in case they get in the way of your game. You don't allow yourself to feel anything that could distract or soften you. Above all, you *never* lower your guard and let anyone see you looking weak. There is no place in a Premier League dressing room for sympathy, and any player stupid enough to show vulnerability will pay for it. What his team mates will see is a weak link – a liability – and nobody wants that on their team. Elite sportsmen are often highly judgemental. They have to be. Premier League culture is harsh, and unforgiving – and it suited me down to the ground.

Even as a child, I didn't show my emotions. People have called me cold all my life. That never bothered me, because all I cared about was winning, and I knew it was the only way. What I did not know, though, was that a mentality which would win me so many medals might not be much use to me in real life. I was about to find out that the tools

4

I had learned to use as a footballer were the last thing my children needed from their dad when tragedy struck.

To see my girl and two boys in so much pain was an agony like nothing I had ever known. To feel helpless to comfort them was worse. They needed me to show them how to grieve for their mum – to manage their sadness, and keep Rebecca's love and memory alive. But in the early days, I just couldn't do it.

I filled my time with an insanely busy work schedule, and numbed my nights by hitting the bottle. I think I would have done literally anything to protect myself from the heart-break. But this was never going to help my kids – and that is why, eventually, I decided to try a different way.

I agreed to make a documentary for the BBC, in which I would meet every sort of grief expert – charities like Child Bereavement UK, a widowed dads' support group, other sportsmen who had been widowed young themselves. To be totally honest, I signed up to it because making the film would force me to see the idea through. Left to my own devices, I could easily see myself getting cold feet. It's one thing to make appointments to meet people who can help. Turning up could be quite another.

The thought that anyone outside our family might watch the programme barely even occurred to me. Back then my only thought was: How will this help my kids? They would be too young to watch the documentary now, but they were the only audience I ever pictured in my mind. When the film was broadcast, I don't think anything could have prepared me for the public response.

More than eight million people watched the documentary

in the first few days, and every day I get strangers coming up to me to tell me how much it moved them. To know that so many learned so much from it was mind-blowing. I would never have guessed how many ordinary blokes – husbands and fathers – are just as much at sea as I am when it comes to our emotions.

Professional footballers are not, I now know, the only ones who have to close down their emotions to be good at their job. From what I've heard from the men who got in touch, all kinds of careers demand the same sort of ruthless detachment. That is the price of professional success. And you won't find much more compassion in most male friendship groups than you do in Manchester United's changing room. When times are good, that isn't a problem. But when the family needs to come first, men find out that what works for them professionally isn't just useless at home, it actually makes matters worse. A heartbroken child needs cuddles and conversation, not a stiff upper lip.

I don't like having to admit I understood none of this when Rebecca died. I hate being wrong. If there had been any way to stick to my guns and help my kids to grieve without exposing my own emotions, I would have taken it. And just because I've now learned some tools and tips, please don't imagine I fancy myself as some sort of grief expert. For me to claim to be an authority would be a joke. I'm still flailing around most of the time, getting it wrong, wishing it wasn't so hard to break old habits and open up. I don't pretend to have all the answers.

However, I've been lucky enough to meet some unbelievably wise people who know the terrain of grief inside out, and can guide people like me through it. If everyone else in the UK could access all the people I met, I probably wouldn't have written this book. But the public response to the BBC documentary showed me the sheer scale of our cluelessness when it comes to dealing with loss. We're all stumbling about in the dark; we all need help.

I've learned something else in the process of making this book. I always knew my memory was terrible – anyone who's ever met me could have told you that. My forgetfulness drives people mad, and I'm not surprised because it really is quite extreme. This book would not have been possible without the assistance of others around me who remember things far more clearly, and to whom I'm very grateful for their contributions. Of course, no two people ever recall events in exactly the same way, and some of those involved in this story will remember it differently from others, but I've done my best to get every detail right.

So, the revelation was not that I'm rubbish at remembering details. No, the shock has been the discovery that there are whole chunks of the story of Rebecca's death which my mind has methodically and deliberately deleted. Critical, life-changing weeks of my life have simply been wiped from my memory. I'm not talking about my normal forgetfulness here, but something quite different. As you will see later in the book, I'm talking about the power of denial, and what the human mind will do to protect itself from reality when reality is literally more than you can bear.

Some of you will read this book as a memoir, and, I hope, enjoy reading the full story of my life with Rebecca, and without her. Other readers may want only practical advice, and use the book more like an instruction manual than a memoir. If you're one of them, you'll find tips and advice in boxes at the end of chapters 10 to 13 (pages 167–70, 193–4 and 207–9 and 221–22).

Rebecca's death has been an unmitigated catastrophe for my family, and for everyone who loved her. Nothing can ever ease the pain, or magic it away. But if I can help anyone else facing what we have gone through, by sharing what I've learned, our loss won't feel completely meaningless. Rebecca never wanted to be in the public eye, and went to any length to protect her anonymity. Making our private life public goes against all my instincts, and sometimes I worry about how she would feel about being in a book. But one thought re-assures me. Rebecca always wanted to help other people. I know she would be glad that, even in death, she still can.

This book is about losing Rebecca, but in the course of writing it, when I thought life had thrown us enough shocks, we suffered another devastating loss. My beloved mother was admitted to hospital with cancer. I could never have imagined that we would have to live through this pain again, but we must. She died on the very day I finished this book. It seems no grief journey can ever really be over.

CHAPTER ONE

Life-changing Moments

IT IS A dark November night in 2000. As I speed home through south London I barely notice the traffic lights ahead. My mind is spinning with thoughts of football, and how my career is about to change.

I've been playing for West Ham since I was fifteen, and have nothing but love and respect for the club. But now Leeds United have just offered to sign me for a British record fee of £18 million. The deal has been agreed. Soon I'll be playing Champions League football, defending against the best strikers in Europe. Leeds is the big-time, the club that is buzzing – and it wants me. The chairman even flew me up there in his private jet. I am twenty-two years old, and on my way.

For a few months, I've been seeing a girl from Essex, called Rebecca. It's still early days, but there's something very different about this relationship. I'm feeling something new for Rebecca, something I've not known with any other girl. Earlier this evening, after signing with Leeds, I had taken her out for dinner to tell her my news. I met her from work in Haymarket, and we went to a restaurant in the West End. I was too excited to eat, and had babbled away across the table at her. Leeds wanted me. I was moving clubs, moving house, moving to Yorkshire. There was so much to do.

I was so wrapped up in it all I didn't even stop to think how the news would hit her.

'Have you agreed to go?' Rebecca had asked. She was very calm.

'Yes, I'm going. I've got to go up tomorrow and that's it.'

'What – you're just going and that's it? Is that how it works?'

'Yes.'

I'd kissed her goodbye, jumped into my car and driven off, already thinking about a thousand other things, all to do with football and none about Rebecca.

It's strange how life-changing moments can happen without you even noticing. Approaching the traffic lights now, I have no idea my future is about to be determined by these little circles of colour. They turn red. I pull up, glance at the car alongside and see it's Rebecca. Messing about, I bib my horn, expecting her to wave and smile. But when she turns her head, I see she's crying.

Until this moment, the thought that she might be upset literally hasn't occurred to me. All I've thought about is football. But there she is, tears streaming down her face, heartbroken. I know they aren't crocodile tears: she couldn't have known we'd meet at the lights and I would see. Had they stayed green, I would have driven on and never known.

And right then, in that second, I know she's coming with

me. I put down the window and call across: 'Are you going to come, or what? What's going on? You coming?'

She calls back, 'I didn't think you were going to ask me. I thought that was it.'

I laugh. 'No. This is it. You're coming.'

LOOKING BACK NOW, we were practically kids, setting off for the north with no real idea what we were doing. We would be there for fourteen years, the first two in Leeds, before I was bought by Manchester United. Our three children were born there: our eldest boy Lorenz, in 2006, his brother Tate in 2008 and their sister Tia in 2011. We won the Premier League title at Man United six times, the Champions League, the League Cup twice and the FIFA Club World Cup. I was capped eighty-one times for England, and captained my country. It was the stuff of dreams, an incredible time.

Ever since I was ten years old, football was all I ever wanted. I used to kick a ball around on a scrap of grass on the south London estate where I grew up, fantasising that it was Wembley. My career as a player gave me everything I could ever have hoped for, and I have no regrets. But there is a price to pay for everything in life, and success on the pitch had to come at the expense of family life.

Rebecca sacrificed everything for my career. She was only eighteen when we got together, and she left behind her friends and family to live in cities where she knew no one. During the season I was barely at home, and even when I was, my mind was still on the pitch, replaying the day's game or training session in my head over and over into the early hours of the morning. Christmas and New Year were always dominated by the big matches, and even in the summer, out of season, I would be away with England or on a foreign pre-season tour. While other families went away together in August, Rebecca and the kids would have to go on holiday with friends or relatives. To the press and the public, she might have looked like a WAG, but in many ways she was more like a single mum.

What kept us going was the knowledge that one day my playing career would be over. All the hard work and sacrifice and separation would be worth it, because once I had retired we would be together as a family. I would be free to be a proper husband to Rebecca, and we couldn't wait.

Some players dread retirement, but they're the ones who didn't plan for it. When their career is over they're lost. I've seen so many get lazy, and I was never going to be one of them. It's not easy if all you're left with is making public appearances for a few hundred quid, when you've been used to earning thousands a week. Everyone has to make a living, and I would never disrespect anyone for the way they find to do it. But I did not want to be another ex-footballer on the after-dinner speaking circuit.

I knew I couldn't sit at home all day either. I've seen a lot of ex-players sink into depression or turn to drink, so I was well aware of the dangers of boredom. There are only so many coffees and lunches you can have with your mates, and I'm not one for golf. I wanted to work.

So, I began planning for retirement when I was twenty-seven or -eight. I opened a restaurant in Manchester called Rosso, and launched an online magazine, *#Five*. Sir Alex

Ferguson, Man United's manager, was not exactly thrilled: he didn't want anything to distract me from my game. But I was fascinated by business, and as retirement approached I put in place a range of projects – a YouTube platform, a production company, a clothing line, a management company. I set up the Rio Ferdinand Foundation, which supports deprived inner-city youngsters, and signed contracts to be a TV pundit. I was feeling optimistic about the future, and confident.

When my time at Man United ended in 2014, I still had a season or two left in me. Players often go abroad to end their career in the US or Far East, but after fourteen years away from London we were ready to go home. Rebecca had been selfless for all these years, but she longed to be back among her friends and family. It was time for her and the family to come first, so I signed with Queens Park Rangers, and we came home.

There was another compelling reason for heading back to London. In 2013 Rebecca had been diagnosed with breast cancer. She had had to undergo a double mastectomy and chemotherapy, and it had been horrible – but the treatment was successful, the doctors seemed confident and we assumed it was behind us. Still, after the shock of an ordeal like that, a kind of primitive homing instinct kicks in, and both of us wanted to be back where Rebecca felt happiest.

I knew from my first day at QPR that it would be my last season. I thought I'd prepared myself for the culture shock of leaving a world-class club for a smaller outfit, but wasn't at all prepared for the mindset of some players at QPR. The media and fans like to accuse top-flight Premier League footballers of caring more about money and glamour than the game, but in fact the professionalism and commitment at a club like Man United is all-consuming. It's in the smaller club dressing rooms that you will hear some of the players talking about nothing but cars, designer clothes, Dubai – basically everything except football. I found it alienating, and maddening. Perhaps, though, it made saying goodbye to the game a little easier. I did not belong in that dressing room; there were better places for me to be now.

In 2010 we had bought a plot of land in Orpington, a suburb of south-east London. It was Rebecca's project, and she poured her heart into building us the perfect family home. She created the dream holiday home for us in Portugal, too, filling it with love and hope for all the future happiness waiting for us there.

For years she had waited patiently for us to be together as a family – and now our time had come. The rest of our life was about to begin.

THERE IS AN old quote that makes a lot of sense to me these days: 'If you want to make God laugh, tell him about your plans.'

In February 2015 Rebecca and her sister took a trip to the house in Portugal together. The pair were always close, so it was a surprise to hear her sister complain when they got back that Rebecca had been unrecognisably snappy, and had spent the whole trip moaning. It wasn't like her at all. I put it down to the back pain she had been mentioning lately, and thought she might have trapped a nerve or slipped a disc or something. It didn't sound like a big deal. I've never been massively sympathetic towards anyone grumbling about aches and pains, so told Rebecca to go to the GP and get it sorted out.

It was the last thing on my mind as I was driving to training with my QPR teammate Bobby Zamora one morning, a week or so later, when my phone rang. It was Rebecca's sister. She sounded semi-hysterical. 'Rebecca's in intensive care. You need to get there now.'

I can't even remember the drive there. My mind was a blur. When I reached the Royal Marsden, Rebecca had been moved to an isolation room to prevent airborne infection, and was lying on her back wired up to every imaginable kind of machine. I was stunned: it looked like a scene from a TV emergency-room drama. She was contorted with pain, too drugged to talk, drifting in and out of consciousness. And yet, even then, it still didn't cross my mind that the culprit in the horror show unfolding before my eyes could be cancer.

Rebecca's mum and dad were there, and her sister. A doctor came to talk to us. We were all shell-shocked, reeling – so much so that it took me a moment to register what the doctor was saying.

'We need to run some urgent tests,' he said, looking grave. 'I'm afraid there's a chance the cancer has come back.'

It had. Within days, I was hearing the worst possible news. The cancer had metastasised to her bones. I tried to take in what the doctors were saying, but their voices became an incomprehensible jangle. They wouldn't be able to cure it, they seemed to be saying, but did hope they could treat it.

I struggled to focus on the words, but they scrambled into a static of distant white noise. I felt like I was falling, tumbling into cold, dark nothingness as I sensed my emotions close down. It was Rebecca who composed herself to speak first.

'Rio, you have to go home and let the kids think everything's normal. Go, let them think everything's normal.'

But nothing was ever going to be normal again. As you will read later, for eight weeks Rebecca fought for her life in that hospital room. Each new drug seemed to offer a glimmer of hope, which I would cling to, willing it to work, refusing to allow the possibility that it might not. I told the children that Mummy was poorly – a bit under the weather – and needed to be in hospital for a little bit while the doctors made her better. I had never allowed myself to entertain the idea that her cancer would ever come back. Surely no one could be that unlucky. Now that it had, I was not about to contemplate the worst.

One cool, windy day in late April, the worst came. The consultant, Mr Johnson, sat opposite me and Rebecca's mum, his expression sombre but kindly, more like a priest's than a medic's.

'We've tried everything we can,' he said softly. 'I'm so sorry.'

I could hear the words, but my mind wouldn't accept them.

'There has to be something else you can try,' I urged. 'There has to be.'

He gazed at me, full of compassion, and shook his head. 'I'm afraid not. She's too weak now. You should go home and tell the children. They need to come and say goodbye to their mum.'

I stared back at him in blank disbelief. My faith in Mr

Johnson was unshakeable. He had done everything he could for Rebecca, and I trusted him entirely. And yet, even so, the impossibility of what he was now telling me to do – the unbearable enormity of it – sparked a flare of irrational anger.

'Right. And how exactly do I tell my kids that?'

The rest of that day is a blur. I know I went straight to the pub and downed a pint of Guinness followed by a brandy. Part of me wanted to numb myself, I think, and part of me was putting off the most difficult thing I had ever had to face. I had always thought of myself as someone who had the steel to step up to a challenge; who always confronted the big moments squarely, who did not lose his nerve. But nothing in my life had prepared me for this.

How do you look into the trusting eyes of your three innocent children, open your mouth and speak words that will shatter their universe and haunt them for the rest of their lives? How could I do that to them? I hadn't the faintest idea.

When the kids woke the next morning, I told them we weren't going to school: we were going to see Mummy instead. As if in a dream, I padded round the kitchen like a sleepwalker, while they chattered away, teasing and squab-bling for all the world as if this were just another ordinary, forgettable day. They had been visiting their mum regularly for weeks, and bounced up the Royal Marsden steps, barrel-ling through the doors as usual, blissfully oblivious to the heartbreak waiting for them inside.

Something like an out-of-body sensation began to seize me as I led them into the room next to Rebecca's. I sat down on a bed that hundreds of people had probably died in. My mum and dad were there, my brother Anton and Rebecca's parents. Everything felt completely unreal, as though we were actors in a movie, impersonating ourselves. Any minute a director was surely going to walk in, shout, 'Cut!' and we could be released from this script and go back to being a happy family. I gazed at my beautiful children, lost for words, searching for a way to begin.

'I'm afraid I've got to tell you something very, very sad. Mum's not going to be able to get out of here. She's got cancer again, and this time she isn't going to get better.' They stared at me, wide-eyed, dumbstruck.

'They've been trying to help her, the doctors, but they can't any more. She's been strong, and she's tried to get better, but I'm so sorry. She's going to be a star – she's going to go up into the stars as a spirit, and she'll always be there in the sky, looking down on us and . . .'

I couldn't go on. Tears were streaming down the children's faces; they were sobbing, crying out.

'Why? Why? Why?' Tate kept wailing, over and over. 'What are you talking about?'

I tried to explain again, but we were beyond words by then, engulfed in a firestorm of pain. Even now, the memory of that scene is enough to plunge me back into a darkness I never want to see again. As the children broke down and sobbed, I held them tight, staring out of the window. All I could think was: Fucking hell, could someone please help me? Please tell me I got that right. I hope they don't come back in ten, twenty years and go, 'The way you described that destroyed me.'

18

We went next door to say our goodbyes. Rebecca had always taken meticulous care to look the best she possibly could for the kids' hospital visits, putting on sweatpants and make-up and trying to sit up and seem normal, but we were way beyond that now. She lay on her back, pale and unconscious, swaddled in a sinister tangle of tubes and wires connected to a bank of medical machinery that beeped and flashed, cold and sterile. I wanted to rip all the wires away to let the children get close enough for one last hug with her all together. Instead, one by one, they took their place at Rebecca's bedside and kissed their mum goodbye.

The tears had subsided into subdued silence by the time we were leaving the hospital. On our way out Tate happened to glance up and spot a big noticeboard on the staffroom wall, plastered with cards.

'What's that, Dad?' he asked.

'Oh, that's where some of the patients and families have left thank-you notes for the doctors and the nurses on the ward, for helping their mum or dad or whoever they've had up there.' He absorbed this in silence, still staring at the wall, as if turning my words over in his mind.

'Well,' he said, coldly 'they didn't help my mum,' and quietly turned and walked away.

Near the door we passed a little cluster of staff. They looked at us. For a moment I made my normal assumption – they're looking at me because I'm a footballer – and stared at the floor. Then it hit me. That's not why they're looking. They know why we're here. The expression on their faces is sympathy; they feel sorry for us. It was a look I was unfamiliar with – who ever feels sorry for a top footballer? – but I was about to have to get used to it.

I barely remember the car journey to Orpington. I can't even remember who drove. Once the kids were settled at home, I made the journey back across London to the Royal Marsden for the final time.

Rebecca will never know she died surrounded by the people who loved her most. I couldn't tell you if she lived for a few more hours after the children had said goodbye, or whether it was the next day, but she never regained consciousness. By then any normal sense of time had become meaningless anyway. At some point, all I know is that I held her arms, with my brother, her mum and dad, brother and sister at her bedside, and together we watched my wife slip away. She was thirty-four years old.

To some people this may sound strange, possibly even macabre, but to me it felt only natural. I slept in Rebecca's bed that night, curled up beside her for one final time, feeling the warmth drain away from her, while her mum slept on a camp bed by the window. I say slept, but I'm not sure either of us did, really. Any sleep to be had was soon hijacked by dreams so surreal that I would wake with a jolt, confused, until the memory of her death blindsided me again. Even so, I would rather have lain there for ever than face the morning when it came, bringing with it all the grim demands of being newly bereaved.

It was May, the month in which I should have been playing my last match as a professional footballer, and beginning the next chapter of my life with Rebecca. Instead, I was about to make arrangements for her body to be collected by undertakers, and go home a single dad to grieving children I was clueless to console. As a footballer I had been equal to anything, and always known what to do. For the first time in my life, I was lost.

Ever since I was a boy, I had always believed my fate lay in my own hands. That if I put in the work – the training, the preparation, the dedication and commitment – I could control my life. I never doubted it. But the truth is that my life with Rebecca – my marriage, my children, my world – began with the chance turn of a traffic light and ended with a random stroke of medical misfortune, stolen by microscopic cancer cells I couldn't even see.

I still don't know how to make sense of this, or what it means. All I knew that day was that it didn't matter how many trophies and medals I had won. They weren't going to help me now.

CHAPTER TWO

Chaos

IT'S EARLY MAY 2015, a few days after Rebecca passed away. I'm at home with the kids. We're late. Not oh-dear-there-won't-be-much-time-to-play-with-your-friends-before-school-starts kind of late. No. We're you've-already-missed-the-class-register-and-we're-not-even-out-the-door late.

The kids haven't been late for school even once in their lives. But, then, they haven't had me in sole charge of the school run before. It feels important to keep them in their normal routine, and I'm trying to get them to school, but this is uncharted territory for all of us – and it isn't pretty. It's pandemonium.

'Dad, where's my PE kit?'

'I don't know, where do you normally keep it?'

'Mum knows where it lives.'

Shit. Shit. Shit. It could be anywhere.

'Dad, this isn't how Mum cooks eggs.'

'Dad, have you got my dinner money?'

'Dad, you've forgotten my pencil case.'

What pencil case? I didn't even know they used the

damned things. I look around frantically. The kitchen is a bomb site. Cereal is scattered all over the counter top. There are egg shells in the sink. Tia's pyjamas are in a ball on the floor.

'Come on, kids, we've got to go – get in the car, now.'

'But, *Dad*!'

I race along the lanes trying not to break the speed limit. I'm used to driving them to school: I've been doing it for years. But it's never normally like this. *What* the fuck is going on?

All eyes are on us as we traipse in late, sheepish and flustered. 'Look at him,' I imagine them whispering. 'It's chaos. He's fucked.'

They are not thinking that at all, really. Of course they're not. But I am.

Because the truth is, it is chaos. And I am fucked.

WHEN A BABY is born, you can't move for leaflets and health visitors and professional advice. Every day someone new shows up at the house to make sure you know what you're doing. Modern society wouldn't dream of leaving a novice parent to work it out as they go along: that would be madness. But when somebody dies, you're on your own.

For the first two weeks after Rebecca died, I wasn't. The house was heaving. Mum moved in; Rebecca's mum moved in; uncles, aunts and cousins seemed to be spilling out of every room. The kettle was always on, a bottle was always open, and never have I been more grateful for the company. It's one of the strange things about death. It brings all the people you love most in the world into your home – except that the one you loved most of all isn't there.

To be honest, I was barely there either. Physically I was present, but mentally I wasn't. I limped from room to room, capsized by the fresh sight of something that belonged to Rebecca – her shoes, a hairbrush, a photograph. Everyone else was trying to organise a funeral, but I could barely tie my own shoelaces. At moments I felt as if I could barely see. I never used to understand the phrase 'blinded by grief' but I did now.

And there were so many decisions to be made. Thank God for Rebecca's parents, who quietly set about making choices – venue, flowers, cars, guest list. Jamie Moralee, my agent and best friend, and his wife Lisa, Rebecca's best friend, seemed to be soldered to the kitchen table, and if they weren't on a laptop they were on the phone. My mum and dad were superhuman, sensing the kids' needs, judging my mood, taking care of business. All I was capable of was choosing the music to be played at Rebecca's funeral.

I still couldn't believe we were actually talking about her funeral. It didn't feel real. Each day I would leave everyone else to it, get into the car and drive to the chapel of rest where she lay. I spent hours at her side, listening to music. Eva Cassidy's 'Songbird' had been our wedding song, and now it was the soundtrack to our goodbye. I played early Mary J. Blige, 'This Woman's Work' by Maxwell, 'My First Love' by Avant. The kids used to sing 'Thinking Out Loud' by Ed Sheeran with Rebecca, and wanted it to be played at the service. She used to dance around the kitchen with them to 'Cheerleader' by OMI, so that would be played too.

'Can we dance to it when it comes on?' they asked.

I thought my heart would break. 'If that's what you want to do, that's what you can do. You can dance.'

Being alone with Rebecca in the chapel of rest in those final days, I found myself wishing we could keep her there for ever. She was cold and still, but even so I would have rather had her there than buried her. One last chance to look at her face kept bringing me back, desperate for more time with her before it was too late. One afternoon, after visiting her, I went and bought as many bottles of her perfume as I could find. She wore Hermès, and I gave the children each a bottle. To this day they still spray their pillows with it. Sometimes I'll walk into Tate's bedroom and the scent is overpowering. I think he must douse his whole bed with it.

Thirteen days after Rebecca died, it was time to say the final goodbye. Her body was brought to the house in a wicker basket for a coffin, carried on a vintage Rolls-Royce hearse. We had decided to ask mourners not to wear black, but to come dressed to celebrate her life. In the sparkling May sunshine the gathering of friends, family and footballers in the driveway, waiting for her body to arrive, would have looked almost festive from a distance, but close up the faces were streaming with tears.

When the children were born Rebecca had made baby blankets for them. Along with notes written by the children, these were what the three of them chose to place in her coffin. I added the poem I had written for her for our wedding. The cortège of cars pulled away, and we set off for the cemetery.

My children sat either side of me throughout the service,

26

but I don't remember any of them shedding a tear. Then we carried her coffin to the grave. After it was lowered into the ground the children scattered petals over it, and the four of us released pink balloons carrying wishes into the sky.

Lorenz was inscrutable, somewhere between solemn and nonchalant. I think neither he nor Tate wanted anyone to see them cry. Tia had only just turned four, and scampered about in her yellow dress, almost as if at a family party. But when the three first saw the freshly dug grave, they were mesmerised.

'So she's going to be in there *for ever*? What about the ants? What about all the insects?'

'Can we get in there? Can we sit down?' They wanted to sit on the edge and swing their legs over.

'What happens to her body? Will it just stay the same? If we pull her out in ten years will she look the same?' It wasn't morbid fascination, but childlike curiosity. They had simply never seen a grave before.

We held the wake at the same pub where Rebecca had celebrated her birthday just six months earlier, in what already felt like another life, another universe. I spent a while circulating, thanking everyone for coming. It felt both necessary and completely bizarre to observe the conventions of normal social etiquette, as if I was hosting some social occasion I actually wanted to be happening. But people had travelled from all over the country, even the world, to be there.

And then I got drunk. I remember DJing at one point – and I remember having a massive go at a cousin I love dearly about something he had done years earlier. 'You make

27

sure you fucking fix up,' I shouted at him. Emotions famously run high at funerals, and I can see why fights even sometimes break out. Everyone is in a heightened state, and the tension must find its release somehow. When the night ended I was rowing with the pub landlord, whose licence I think ended at eleven p.m. He offered to keep going until one o'clock, but I was having none of it. 'What are you talking about? I'm not stopping.' I have no idea how long we kept the wake going, but it was certainly well into the early hours.

I didn't want it to end because I knew what was coming next. Right up until the day of the funeral, a death feels not exactly finite – but you are focused on a date, an end point. But when that day is over, that isn't the end at all. It's just the beginning. The heartbreak stretches into eternity, with no prospect of closure.

And everyone leaves. They have to: they have lives to go back to. I had been to enough funerals myself to know that as a guest you show up, you feel sad, then you leave – and five minutes later you can be smiling about something. You're on the phone to a mate, saying, 'Right, I'll meet you in an hour for a few pints.' Because your life goes on. Nothing has really changed.

But when you have just buried your wife, you're not going to forget and move on. Not now, and not ever. You're facing a life sentence of sadness, and you're facing it alone.

IT IS DISORIENTING, and very humbling, to be one of the best in the world at what you do for a living – and then discover you're a total amateur in your own house. In the early weeks after the funeral, I began to see just what it takes to run a family home. A lot more than I'd ever guessed, as I quickly discovered. I didn't have a clue what I was doing.

Washing-machines, tumble-driers, dishwashers, the number for the guy who services the boiler, the name of the house-insurance company – all were a total mystery to me. How did any of it work? A home that used to run like clockwork was now dysfunctional beyond belief. Our old housekeeper from Manchester, Sandra, had moved in when Rebecca was admitted to the Royal Marsden; she agreed to carry on living with us, thank God, and my mum was a lifesaver too. It wasn't just that I needed them on a practical level: there was also something very soothing about having two calm older women in the house who had known the children all their lives. I know how lucky I am to have had – and still have – so much help. But ultimately it was down to me to take charge, and in the early days you might as well have put a toddler at the wheel of a bus.

I used to think I was a brilliant dad for driving my kids to school. I would hear mums moan about the school run and think, What's their problem? It's easy. What I didn't know was that it was easy because Rebecca did the 99 per cent I didn't even see.

In the morning, the kids always had to be at school for eight a.m. Rebecca would wake them up at six fifteen, get them dressed and ready, and they would be downstairs by seven at the latest. They'd eat a proper cooked breakfast, and be ready to go by seven forty-five. The night before, she would have prepared PE kits, school bags, lunch money, homework; she'd have been in touch with other mums about playdates; she'd have checked the after-school-club calendar. And me? I would get out of bed and swan downstairs at about five to eight. The kids would get into the car, and I'd drive off, congratulating myself on being Superdad.

I had no idea that she was thinking and planning and organising twenty-four hours a day. Being a mum is all about preparation – and if you don't get it right, everything quickly falls apart.

All this came as a total shock. I didn't even know who the kids' GP or dentist was. I hadn't seen a GP myself since I was fourteen years old. As a professional footballer you see the club doctor, but now that I was retired I didn't even know how to set about registering with a surgery. The first time I needed an appointment, I just rang the QPR doctor on autopilot.

'Er, Rio,' he had to explain kindly, 'you don't play for the club any more. I'm not your doctor now.'

On top of getting to grips with domestic appliances and the school timetable, there was the whole business of the kids' social life. Who knew their diaries were so busy? As if getting them to school wasn't hard enough, I'd arrive in the playground and have half a dozen mums asking, 'Can we take Tate for a playdate on Friday?' or 'Would you have so-and-so to yours to play with Tia on Tuesday?' All I wanted to do was drop the kids and run – but you have to engage with the social whirlwind, or your kids are going to be Billy No Mates. It's intense, and relentless.

When you're used to knowing exactly what you're doing, it's also very daunting. The fear of getting it wrong haunted me, because children have no filter and will let you know in no uncertain terms when you mess up. 'What's this?' Lorenz would demand, pointing to his plate at supper time. 'That's not right. Where's Mummy's chicken?' I didn't know Rebecca's little bedtime routines – the way she'd tuck them in, or how they liked the night light left – and every time one of the kids put me right, it was hard not to take the correction as a criticism, even though I knew they hadn't meant to hurt me.

When Rebecca was alive I never had to worry about whether I was getting anything right or wrong with the kids. I had only to glance at her, and I would know. She was always there as a safety net. With that safety net gone, I was vulnerable suddenly, and full of self-doubt.

Rebecca had always seemed miraculously confident as a mum. Even when it came to the kids' clothes, she had a knack for knowing what worked. If a dress from Tesco looked better on Tia than some designer outfit from Gucci, Rebecca didn't think twice about putting her in the Tesco dress for a party. She loved taking the children to Dubai, but at other times she would take them off to Center Parcs or a caravan park in Wales. She had regimented routines for homework, bedtime, the school run, but always knew how to turn everything into a game. On a boiling hot day one summer, when I was still at Man United, she got the kids dressed up in Puffa jackets and snow boots and took them to an indoor snow centre called the Chill Factor. They had a ball snowboarding and skiing while everyone outside was melting in the heat. Rebecca just knew how to get the right balance between routine and discipline, fun times and treats. It was as if she had the magic formula. To me it was all a mystery.

Lorenz and Tate's ninth and seventh birthdays fell within three months of her death. Did I buy them too many presents – or not enough? Would Rebecca have chosen something different? Would she have approved of what the boys got? It was impossible to know. But that didn't stop me endlessly second-guessing and fretting. I questioned myself and everything I did as a dad. Rebecca had always said she didn't want Tia to have her ears pierced too young – but what did that mean? What was 'too young'?

On the very first Christmas without Rebecca, after opening presents I took them to the cemetery to wish their mum a happy Christmas. The children had made cards for her, and brought flowers, and seemed curiously upbeat and relaxed there. After leaving the cards and flowers on her grave, they charged about on the grass as if we were in a park. I sat by her headstone and broke down. I couldn't believe this was where we were. No child should have to be in a cemetery on Christmas Day. Was it right to bring them? I just didn't know.

In some ways the kids remained as recognisable to me as they always had. Tia has always reminded me of Rebecca. Like her mum, she can enjoy being girly and spend hours playing around with her hair – but she's also a bit of a tomboy, and loves haring around on her bike with her brothers. She's formidably single-minded, exactly like Rebecca: once Tia has decided she doesn't want to do something, that's usually that. 'No, I *told* you,' she'll chide, arms firmly folded, if I try to talk her round. 'I *don't* want to.'

Tate reminds me of myself. He's quite a handful – boisterous, loud, mischievous – and his school reports read exactly like mine used to: 'Tate is very capable and has the ability to achieve the goals that are set for him. But he is easily distracted – and easily distracts others.' That's Tate – and me – in a nutshell.

Lorenz is way better behaved than I ever used to be. Self-contained and quite serious, though he can be funny too, he likes to think things through for himself, and will walk away from confrontation rather than allow himself to be provoked or cause a scene. But I recognise in him that innate sense of responsibility that comes with being the eldest child, and he wants to impress just as I used to.

The kids had not undergone any dramatic change since their mum's death. But the mystery – the question going round and round in my mind, tormenting my days and haunting my nights – was: how are they feeling? From the day I told them she was dying in hospital, they seemed weirdly blank, getting on with their lives almost as if nothing had happened. I knew they couldn't possibly be okay – obviously they couldn't – but I didn't know what was going on inside their heads. What were they thinking? What were they feeling? It was impossible to tell.

When Rebecca was first diagnosed with breast cancer, she had told me how she thought the kids would react if she didn't survive. At the time I couldn't contemplate the possibility, so paid little attention, but her predictions were now proving uncannily accurate. Tia, she had said, would be too young to absorb the enormity of the loss – and she was right. Only four when her mum died, Tia would exclaim, 'Oh, Mummy would have liked to hear this song,' if she heard one of Rebecca's favourite tracks, and would happily babble about how she used to dance to it with her mum. But from the way she said it you'd have thought Rebecca had just popped to the shops for a pint of milk.

Sometimes Tia would look for 'Mummy's star' in the sky at bedtime. If cloud cover was low and no stars could be seen, she would start to cry. Without fail, the boys would turn on her.

'Why are you crying like that? Why you crying?'

'Because I can't see Mummy's star.'

'Dad, tell Tia to stop crying. Make her stop crying.' The boys wouldn't dream of comforting her: they just wanted the crying to stop.

Rebecca had been most worried for Tate. 'He's this bouncy little whirlwind of hustle-bustle, and he can be so in your face. But he's got a soft centre, and he's the one who would be more emotional.' Again, she was right. Tate was cuddly, and would come and sit in my lap or lie on my chest. But whenever I asked him what he was thinking he would look angry and blank the question. And Lorenz? Lorenz was a total enigma.

'Lorenz would be a closed book. He'd keep his feelings to himself,' Rebecca had said. Not once since breaking the news to the children in hospital did I see Lorenz cry again. With only two years between them, he and Tate have always been fiercely competitive. Tate is as tall as his brother, so fancies his chances against Lorenz at everything from races to football to fights. Lorenz will cry if he loses – but about his mum? I didn't see one tear. Often he would quietly take himself off to his room and play by himself, and if he saw me weep when we visited Rebecca's grave he would look embarrassed, almost faintly appalled. 'Are you *crying*?' He showed not one flicker of emotion. At the cemetery he would stare down at her grave, deep in thought, but whenever I asked what he was thinking, he would just shrug. 'Oh, nothing.' I couldn't work him out at all.

One of the few hints to what was going on beneath the

surface in the kids came in the form of anxiety about getting on an aeroplane. Lorenz went from being a boy who wanted to be a pilot when he grew up to becoming a terrible flier – fidgety, anxious and fretful. He would get agitated as we reached the gate, and throughout the flight he would be constantly looking around, checking everything out. Whenever I went abroad for work he would pester me: 'What type of plane are you going on, Dad? What's the make? What's the model?'

Something else I noticed was that the boys began to make a meal out of the tiniest bumps and scrapes. Before Rebecca died, they'd always been the kind of kids who would take a tumble and pick themselves straight up, brush themselves off and keep going. Now the slightest knock could have them howling and hopping around, like— Well, I was going to name a few footballers notorious for taking dives, but I won't. It was as if a bang on the elbow gave them an alibi to let out some of the distress they felt unable to express in any other way.

The children had never lost anyone important to them before their mother. They hadn't even experienced the death of a pet. I suspected Rebecca's death had hit Lorenz hardest of all: he had been her firstborn, and there is a special bond between a mum and her eldest that nothing can ever compete with or replace. Rebecca was the only person Lorenz had ever been tactile and cuddly with – yet nobody looking at him now would have been able to guess what he was suffering. He was cold and smooth, like a glacier.

Some of the hardest times were during meals in restaurants.

I would watch the kids study other tables, staring at families that had both a mum and a dad. I could see them analysing, speculating, watching. But every time I tried to get them to tell me what they were thinking, it was always the same story.

'Nothing, Dad.'

One lunchtime in Portugal, three months after Rebecca died, I took the kids to a little bistro in the marina. We arrived early, and the restaurant was still quiet, but as we were looking at menus a family took a table across from ours on the terrace. They were British, with two boys about the same age as mine. One had burned his shoulders in the sun, and Tia watched his mum search through their bags, then tenderly smooth cream over his skin while he wriggled and yelped.

Tia turned to me. 'Dad. Why haven't I got a mum?'

My heart seized. 'Mummy wasn't well, sweetheart. She was strong, and she tried to fight the cancer, but she was unlucky. When the cancer says you've got to go, it takes you.'

In a flash, Lorenz changed the subject. 'Dad! They've got calamari! Can I have calamari?'

Tia tried again. 'But why did it have to take *my* mum?'

Tate jumped in: 'Dad! Look!' He pointed towards the promenade. 'There's that man advertising the boat trips! Can we book one? Can we go this afternoon?'

I always used to think I could handle whatever life threw at me. And maybe I'm deluding myself, but had Rebecca's death been my loss alone, I think I could have found a way to cope. But when I watched my kids lose their mother, and was helpless to comfort them or know what they needed – that was more than I could bear.

I used to read about widowers driven to suicide by grief, and think, You selfish, selfish bastard. I thought they were weak, and Rebecca would have said the same. If anyone had told me I would ever experience an urge to end my own life I would have told them they were mad. I wasn't a coward. That would never be me. And yet, within a week of Rebecca's funeral, I found myself sitting downstairs in the middle of the night, seeing how easy it would be to feel that way. I never actually considered killing myself, not for a minute. Suddenly, though, for the first time I could see how tempting it would be to bring an end to the unbearable agony of grief.

There were moments, too, when in my despair I told myself, Why not just get in the car and drive? Drive as far as you can, as fast as you can, and see if you can somehow flee this torment. The only escape fantasies I had ever entertained before had come after particularly humiliating defeats on the football pitch. If we lost a cup final I longed to run away and hide, ideally on a desert island – somewhere where no one would know about the match, or ask me stupid questions about it, or say anything, or even look at me.

Now I found myself wondering, Could I run away from all this, even for just a week? What would everyone think? Would my kids ever be able to understand and forgive? No, I'd look weak. It would be unconscionable. I could never do that. Okay, then, how about we all run away together? Yes, that could work. But hang on a minute, Rio, get real. You can hardly even get them out the door to school in the morning. How do you think you're going to get them to a desert island?

These were the crazy thoughts going round and round in my head every night. So I escaped the only way I knew how – with drink. Every night I would take a bottle to bed with me, or tell Sandra I was turning in, then wait until she'd gone to bed and creep back downstairs to drink into the early hours. I drank beer, whisky, brandy – a lot of brandy – anything, really. It was the only way I knew how to numb my heart and slow the panic in my mind. I don't even know how long the drinking went on for. One day morphed into another in a blur of alcohol.

Of course, whatever I might have told myself, I wasn't fooling anyone. Sandra could see how much I was drinking from the empty bottles stacking up in the recycling every morning. My family were aware of it, too – and had it gone on for much longer, I imagine someone would have had a word. But before anyone had to, I came to my senses. It was sink-or-swim time. This wasn't me, and it certainly wasn't going to make me happy. Drink could numb the pain for a night – but when I woke the next morning it would still be waiting for me, toxic and cold in the pit of my stomach. There had to be another way.

I thought I knew what it was. I'd throw myself headlong into work.

'Jamie, mate,' I told my agent, 'fill my diary. Seriously, I mean *fill* it. I do not want a single second of the day left unaccounted for. Hire me a PA, get me out on the road – I want to be as busy as it's humanly possible to be. Every second I'm not looking after the kids, I want to be working.'

And, for a while, it helped. All the plans Jamie and I had made for my retirement went into turbo charge, and gave me a refuge from the heartache. But just like suicide, or running away, or drink, workaholism could never be a healthy solution, just another version of an attempt to escape. More to the point, it was never going to help my children get through the death of their mother. If they were ever going to come to terms with their loss, they needed to grieve properly. And how could they learn to do that if I couldn't show them?

The summer after Rebecca died, we went to the house in

Portugal. I arrived ahead, without them. As I turned the key and walked through the door I saw a plaque she'd bought and hung in the hall. It read: 'This Is Our Happy Ever After'. I crumpled to the floor as if someone had swung a baseball bat at me.

'You know, kids,' I told them during that holiday, while they were messing about in the pool one afternoon, trying to do back flips, 'sometimes I cry, you know, on my own, and stuff like that. Do any of you lot cry when you're on your own?' They stopped splashing and turned to look at me.

'Yes,' they all said. 'Yes.'

'Where do you cry?'

'When we're in bed, by ourselves. Because sometimes we miss her.'

Finally, I thought. At last we're going to start to talk about how we feel. We're going to open up, and help each other to grieve.

Who was I kidding? There was one moment that summer in Portugal when Tate broke down and wept. I'm still not really sure why it happened at that particular moment. We were out in the garden together, just the two of us, and I asked, 'How you feeling? You all right? Do you miss Mummy?' He turned to look at me, and tears began to stream down his cheeks. Climbing into my lap, he howled.

'Yes. I just miss her. I miss my mum. I miss my mum.' I took him in my arms and he sobbed and sobbed as I held him tightly.

And after that . . . nothing. The more I tried to get the kids to open up and talk, the more they closed down and shut me out. They hated me trying, and it got to the point when if I mentioned Rebecca and asked Lorenz if he missed her, he would just get to his feet, ask coldly, 'Can I go now?' and walk away.

I asked the people around me for advice. 'Oh,' everyone said. 'Don't worry. Car journeys will do the trick. They'll open up on car journeys.' Trust me, I wasn't getting anything out of them in the car. 'Oh, well, then, at the breakfast table,' they said. 'Families always talk at the breakfast table.'

They do? Not mine. All I was getting at the breakfast table was: 'You don't make eggs the way Mum used to.'

Although the children weren't talking to me about their mum, there were moments when they would open up a tiny little bit to others. The night Rebecca died, while I was lying beside her body in the hospital, Sandra slept in Tia's bed and held her while she cried out for her mum. The following day Tate asked Sandra to make a little flower bed in the garden for his mum. He chose forget-me-nots to plant with her.

One night, in bed in Portugal, that first summer without Rebecca, Tate broke down in tears when Sandra came to say goodnight. 'Why does cancer exist?' he asked. 'What is it? Why did it take Mum? I wish Mum was still here.' Sandra held him and soothed him until he fell asleep in her arms.

It wasn't much, in the face of the enormity of their loss. But it was something. And yet with me – nothing.

I was more than just their dad now. I had to be their mum and dad – and I had to learn how to help them. I would have given anything to find a way to open them up. But I was asking them to do something I had never known how to do myself.

I couldn't blame them for keeping their feelings locked away. How could I? Not when they had seen me do exactly that with mine all their lives.

CHAPTER THREE

Growing Up

IT'S A WEEKDAY morning in 1987, in our flat on an estate in Peckham. I'm nine years old. I'm in the bathroom, having a shower, and my dad's brushing his teeth. I have a little brother, Anton, but he is only two and still in bed. My dad has something to tell me, but he offers it so casually I take it to mean next to nothing.

'Listen,' he says, still brushing his teeth. 'I'll be gone for a little while. I'm not going anywhere, I'm just moving to the next estate.'

It sounds like he's maybe taking a break and he'll be back soon. 'Oh, all right. That's all right, Dad, cool,' I say. 'See you later.' The biggest moment in my life has just happened – and I don't realise it. I go off to school without giving it another thought.

As the days become weeks, and the weeks become months, and my dad still doesn't come back, I try to find out what's going on. He's been staying at his brother's, but now he's moved into his own flat. I go round, and he's laying new floors, decorating the walls, fitting a kitchen.

'So are you staying here now, Dad?' I ask him.

He doesn't even look up. Head bent, hammering a nail, he mumbles, 'Ask your mother.' That's all he'll ever tell me: 'Go and ask your mother.' I try, but my mum refuses to talk about it too.

That's how it is in my family.

TO UNDERSTAND WHY I found it so hard to grieve properly for Rebecca, you need to know how I was brought up. Don't get me wrong, I had a very happy childhood, and it stood me in great stead for life as a professional footballer. But to say we didn't like to talk about our feelings in my family would be, well, something of an understatement.

Dad was the seventh of ten children, and was born in St Lucia. When he was two years old his parents moved to London to work, leaving their children to be raised by their maternal grandmother. This arrangement is not unusual for post-colonial Caribbean families, and the first decade of my dad's life was full of love, light and laughter. Everyone knew who he was and looked out for him, and some of his happiest memories are of knocking about in rural St Lucia, barefoot and free. But when he turned ten, his parents sent for their children – and all of a sudden, just like that, Dad's childhood was over. He and his siblings found themselves living in a cold, dank two-bedroom flat in south London with a couple who were essentially total strangers to them.

After moving to England, his parents had had another son, Dad's youngest brother. But they also had twins who died. Their death was never spoken of, or even mentioned. As Dad says, 'They kept things to themselves.' But maybe the tragedy played a part in explaining the dark, angry family atmosphere he found waiting for him in England.

To be fair, his father's approach to parenting wasn't unheard of for a West Indian man of his generation. By the standards of today, though, it would look hair-raising, if not land him in prison. He had been a policeman in St Lucia, and became a teacher in London, which must have suited his authoritarian streak. In St Lucia he had been used to commanding respect. Dad thinks he must have found his new status as a lowly immigrant in London difficult to come to terms with, and maybe he took out his resentment on his children.

Family life involved no love, but revolved instead around commands, chores and church. It was a horrible shock for my dad. So was being called a 'black bastard' in the street. It would have been unthinkable, though, for Dad to talk about the racism and his unhappiness with his parents. Traditional Caribbean parenting culture had no place for that sort of thing. My granddad preferred beatings to conversations.

My grandmother was one of twelve, nine of whom had moved to London, but they were no source of comfort or support for my dad. Sometimes when they visited and witnessed the beatings, they would say, 'Oh, Ferdinand, leave the kids alone.' But they never intervened – and there was nobody at school Dad trusted enough to confide in. He was nearly eleven years old, in a strange country, and felt utterly alone.

Within six months, my dad had become violent. Angry

and rebellious, he took out his rage at school, and started getting into regular fights. At thirteen, he quit school. By then one of his older brothers was eighteen, and had begun working in the rag trade, so my dad simply joined him. He worked in a clothes factory, and spent his wages on clothes. My dad has always cared a lot about what he wears; in his late fifties now, he is still always impeccably dressed, and a very handsome guy. He looks so young, people often take us for brothers.

At fourteen, he bought himself a beautiful white suit with black velvet lapels, and a Chinese silk print shirt. He hid them under his bed at home. But his father found them, and threw them out of the window. My dad saw red, the pair fought, and Dad stormed out.

At four thirty the following morning, when my dad had come home and was asleep, his father crept up on him in bed and set about him with a broomstick. Dad woke to a volley of blows, his father livid with fury as he thrashed him. He broke my dad's arm.

But that was not what hurt my dad most. It was his mum rushing into the room, seeing the commotion, and not protecting her son but telling him, 'Go! Get out of here! Go!'

Dad looked at her in disbelief. 'What do you mean, I should go? Why don't you tell him to go? He's the one causing the problem.'

His mum shook her head. 'No, I think you should go.'

So he did. And from that day onwards, Dad always said he felt nothing – *nothing* – towards his mother. She was dead to him. Her betrayal was life-changing, and he never forgave her. For the next few months he lived in relatives' spare rooms and on couches. Then he moved in with a friend and his father. He never went home to his parents again.

My mum came from another family with its own traumas and heartbreaks. Her paternal Irish grandparents both died tragically young, leaving her dad to grow up in a London children's home. He hated the home, and ran away in his teens, stowing away on a ship and getting himself a job in the dockyards on the Thames. Mum's mother came from Yorkshire, and after they met the couple set up home on a council estate in Bermondsey, then a deprived neighbourhood just south of the river. They had six children, of whom my mum was the fourth.

One afternoon, when my mum was eight, she came home from school to find the front door shut and her mother nowhere to be seen. She sat on the doorstep with her siblings and waited. When it began to get dark they went and knocked on the doors of their mum's friends, but no one had seen her. They came home and huddled on the doorstep until finally they heard their dad's footsteps: he was coming home from his shift as a forklift driver. Surprised to find his children locked out, he brought them inside – and this was what they found.

On a table was a note their mother had left, written on a page she'd torn from one of their school exercise books. 'I've taken all I need,' it said. And that was it. No explanation, nothing – just that. In shock, the kids broke down in tears. Their dad wept too. Then he cooked them Spam fritters. Afterwards, they went to bed and cried themselves to sleep. My mum says that, as she fell asleep that night, she felt as if she was falling off a cliff. For the rest of her childhood, that feeling never left her.

Her mum never came home, and her dad brought their six kids up alone. He was an amazing man, solid and decent, and would dash home from work in his lunchbreak to make the kids' supper so it would be ready when they got home from school. They lived off Provident cheques, and never had enough money for my mum to have the right school uniform. Mind you, her schooling was pretty patchy: she bunked off so much that in the end it was usually easier to start at a new school than try and catch up at the old one. Then she'd bunk off again, until another new school would take her, and so it went on.

Her dad took care of his kids' practical needs, and he did a proper job of it. But there was no one to take care of Mum's emotional needs. She had no one to talk to about how she felt about anything – and so she taught herself not to need it.

My mum isn't a talker: she's a doer, a survivor. For her whole life she hasn't wanted to talk about her mother. She never found out why she walked out, but thinks now that she must have been suffering from depression. Until the day he died, her dad would not say a bad word about her mum, and Mum thinks perhaps this was because he knew she wasn't herself when she left.

Mum did meet her again, just once, when she was eighteen. By then her mum was running a pub in the West End – she was a big drinker, and probably an alcoholic – and sent a message for Mum to come and see her. It was a cold, uncomfortable encounter. She didn't want to talk about what had happened, or apologise, or explain, and Mum walked away feeling dead towards her, knowing they would never meet again. They did almost cross paths many years later, by accident, when Mum was visiting a pub in south London run by one of her brothers, Tony. By then a few of the siblings were trying to have some kind of relationship with their mother, and as my mum was leaving the pub one of her brothers arrived with her.

'Oh, is that Tony's wife?' Mum heard her say to my uncle.

'No,' he had to correct her. 'That's your daughter.'

When she died earlier this year, my mum did not go to her funeral.

If you were to ask my mum, I think she would say she was looking for some sort of family of her own ever since her mother left – and when she was fourteen, she met my dad. He was sixteen, and they met in a nightclub called the Butts near the Elephant and Castle in south London. He clocked her as soon as he walked in – she was slim, good-looking, with long blonde hair – and asked his friend who she was. His friend told him she was going out with a guy my dad particularly disliked. Dad spent the evening watching her, then turned to his friend. 'I'm going to have this girl,' he said.

They began going out. Mum wasn't bowled over by him, and if you were to ask her why she'd say it was because he was 'always busy doing his own thing'. It wasn't until I was an adult that I came to understand that she meant Dad just wasn't ready to settle down and fully share his life. After about a year he moved house again, this time to live with another friend and his family, and not long afterwards Mum more or less moved in too. She was only fifteen, and had finally found what felt like a real family to her. The mother was an extraordinary woman: she had five sons of her own, but was always taking in other kids in trouble or needing somewhere to stay. My mum became a kind of daughter to her, and it was from her that Mum learned how to be a woman and a mother herself.

Mum was just eighteen and working at Topshop when she fell pregnant with me. She was thrilled. My dad was not. He was a good-looking young guy, living for music, nightclubs and clothes. I don't think nappies and night feeds exactly figured in his dreams. Mum got them a council flat in Peckham, a poor, rough south London neighbourhood, and slowly she built herself a friendship group of other mums she could rely on. At the end of each week they would all have run out of money so they pooled what food each had left, then cooked and ate together to get them through to the next cheque.

It must have been unimaginably tough for my mum. She adored being a mum, but when I was very young, Dad would come home on a Friday night with his wages, get dressed up, go out and not be seen again until Sunday. Mum would pretend to everyone that he was home all weekend, because she couldn't bear anyone to feel sorry for her. I think her phobia about sympathy traces back to being abandoned by her mother. At some deep, wordless level she must have felt humiliated, and other people's concern didn't help but only reinforced her sense of shame. It was a primitive survival instinct, I guess – and one which I have, as you will see, inherited.

But, of course, like all kids, I took the circumstances of my childhood for granted, never wondering how my parents felt about their life. It was years before I learned the full story of their own family backgrounds, and the hardships they had faced.

We lived on a massive sprawling estate called the Friary, at 18 Gisburn House, surrounded by all the usual council-estate clichés – fighting, shouting and late-night drunken mayhem. One night, a girl I knew was stabbed to death on a stairwell in the block next to mine, which shook the estate badly, but I don't think they ever found out who killed her. In 2000 one of the most notorious murders of modern times took place in another stairwell on a neighbouring estate: a 10-year-old boy called Damilola Taylor was knifed in the thigh by some older kids and left to bleed to death.

Back then you could find every colour, culture and creed on my estate, and I grew up around Irish boys, Turkish boys, African boys, Caribbean boys. For all our differences, we were a surprisingly integrated community. Even so, it was still the 1980s, when racism was rife, and my mum, as a white woman, had to deal with a lot of hostility for being with a black man. She didn't like to talk about it much – but when the racism was directed towards her son, I got to see exactly how she dealt with it.

One evening I was riding home from football when I turned a corner on the estate and a woman kicked me clean off my bike. From thirty yards away, my mum saw. Like a hurdler she flew over a fence, and came sprinting up to the woman. 'Don't you ever, *ever* fucking touch my kid again,' she screamed, and punched the hell out of her.

Another time I was playing outside on the landing and heard a woman call out of her window: 'There's that fucking nigger again.'

I went inside to my mum. She was busy in the kitchen so I stood at the door and asked, 'What does nigger mean?' She froze. Turning to look at me, her cheeks colouring, she said very quietly, 'What?'

I repeated my question.

'Who said that? Who's told you that word?' she demanded. She sounded dangerously cold.

'The woman next door. I heard her say, "There's that nigger again."'

'Get inside,' Mum ordered, and stormed out of the door. I followed her, half scared, half curious. She strode along the landing, hammered on the neighbour's door, and when the woman opened it, my mum grabbed her by the throat, yanked her out and beat the crap out of her.

Eventually Mum left Topshop and took a childminding job at the One O'Clock Club on our estate, which meant she was always around. She couldn't afford to pay for me and my brother to go to clubs, but couldn't bear for us to miss out on opportunities available to other kids, so she used to volunteer everywhere – youth clubs, the adventure play-ground, drama groups – in return for free membership for us. When we weren't at a club with Mum, I would be out with my mates on the estate playing football. I would know it was time to come in when I'd hear her yell from the balcony, 'Reeee-oh! Reee-oh!' Once I'd heard my name, there was no hanging about: if I wasn't indoors within two minutes, I'd get a clip around the ear.

Me, aged 12

My dad was less physically present, but mattered more to me than anyone or anything. He worked as a tailor with two of his brothers, hand-cutting clothes all over north and east London, and had usually left for work before I woke up. He was seldom home before six thirty or seven in the evening, and would often head straight back out again. I was always desperate to go with him, just to spend some time with him, but too scared to ask. 'Ask Dad if I can come with him in the car?' I would beg my mum.

'Why don't you ask him yourself?' she would say. But as much as I loved my dad, I was also terrified of him.

When he was home he loved to play vintage reggae and soul, which he taped off pirate radio stations. Some evenings his mates would come round to smoke and chat and listen to music. I was always desperate to sit with them, but usually wasn't allowed. Occasionally, he would let me – but I knew better than to open my mouth. If I spoke a word when his friends were in the house he would turn on me with a dangerous edge in his voice that told me it was time to leave. He made it very clear that in the company of adults it was not a child's place to start chatting.

At weekends he used to do security work on the doors of pubs and clubs, and wouldn't get home before dawn on a Sunday morning. My brother and I would try not to disturb him, but we were only kids and would forget and start messing about. Then I would hear my dad get out of bed and fetch his belt, and all hell would break loose. One time my dad beat me so hard, my mum jumped on his back, screaming at him to stop, trying to pull him off me.

If you provoked him, he would blow without warning. When we were out in the car and another driver called out something racist, my dad would pull over, cold as ice, get out and stride up to him. I would watch in the rear-view mirror as he tried to pull the other driver out and have a confrontation. Afterwards he would get back in the car without saying a word, and we would drive on as if nothing had happened.

To my dad, violence must have seemed perfectly normal. Compared to his own father, he was practically a pacifist. On Saturday afternoons I used to go round to his parents' flat, which would always be full of cousins and uncles. It was noisy, cramped and chaotic, and I used to love hanging out and feeling part of a big rowdy tribe. But one Saturday my granddad hit one of my cousins – and for my dad that was enough. He knew what our grandfather was capable of, and stopped us visiting for fear of what we might see there.

If my dad was always a bit afraid of his father, my friends were in turn terrified of my dad. When they knocked at the door, asking for me to come out to play, he would growl and slam it in their faces. 'Tell your pals they need to learn to say "please" and "thank you",' he would bark at me.

'But we did!' they'd complain when I talked to them. 'Your dad's just too raw, man, he's too raw.' They soon learned never to knock on my door unless they knew my dad was out.

Between my parents I never saw one shred of affection. They never kissed or held hands, or even sat side by side; in the living room they would always take opposite sofas. Not once did I ever hear one say, 'I love you,' to the other. They didn't say it to me either. To this day, my dad has never told me he loves me. I know he does, of course, and suspect he might even want to say it. As I've got older I've taught myself to end phone calls to him with 'I love you', and I bet he secretly likes it, but all I hear in the silence down the line is embarrassment. After an awkward pause he will usually mumble something like, 'Okay then, see you later.'

You may by now have formed the impression that my early life was loveless and traumatic. I know we're all prone to get misty-eyed with nostalgia when it comes to our own childhood, but I can honestly say that my early life on the estate felt like paradise to me. In those days kids were allowed to play out by themselves, and everyone got along together. There was always someone to kick a ball about with – you could never be lonely.

I was seven when my brother Anton was born. You might imagine I felt jealous towards this interloper stealing my mum and dad's attention, but in fact it felt nothing but good to me to have someone else in the family. The other families on the estate tended to be big, and now I had my own partner in crime. Looking back I can see I must have seemed impossibly grown-up to Anton, and gilded with big-brother glamour, but I don't think I realised it at the time. I was too busy teasing and testing him, trying to make him stronger, fitter and better at football.

If he was kicking a ball around with a friend, I'd go in goal. 'Play two on one,' I'd shout, but I'd let his mate beat me and score, just to make Anton hungrier to win.

'You let that goal in!' Anton would scream, practically in tears.

'No, I didn't!' I'd yell back, straight-faced but laughing inside. Big brothers always take liberties, and I was no different, but making him a better player meant everything to me. As we

With my brother Anton

got older it must have been hard for him to always be 'Rio's brother', but we've stayed tight and he's always known I have his back.

Back then I thought of myself as the luckiest boy on the estate, because my parents lived together. I was one of only a couple of kids there who had the luxury of two parents under one roof, and I felt both blessed and intensely proud.

Moments with my dad brought me the purest happiness I knew. It did not happen very often, but occasionally my dad would let me snuggle up beside him on the sofa while he was watching television. I would cuddle up in the crook of his arm, gazing at the screen, thinking, *This is the best.*

IT WAS ANYTHING but the best for Mum, though. My dad would be the first to admit that he was not ready to be a father or a family man back then. He was still too absorbed in himself, too tied up in his own pursuits and choices. Eventually my mum could take it no longer and, to everyone's amazement – because of course, she hadn't breathed a word to anyone about her unhappiness in the relationship – she told him to leave.

I don't think my parents' separation particularly affected me at first. My dad moved to the neighbouring Yellow Brick Estate, and almost immediately he seemed to soften. He began taking me and my brother out with him, and made more of an effort with us. But after a few months, as I watched him renovate his new flat, the penny slowly dropped: he was not coming back. All he would say when I wanted to know why was: 'Ask your mother. Your mother doesn't want me.'

All she would say was 'I'm not talking about it.'

She was following her own father's example: he wouldn't say a bad word to his children about their mother, even though she had walked out, and Mum would never criticise Dad to us. But I did what kids always do when they're left in the dark. I was too young to be able to see that he might not have been an ideal partner so I jumped to the wrong conclusion. I assumed that, because the separation was Mum's decision, it was her fault. She had broken up our family. I was no longer the lucky kid on the estate whose parents were together, I was furious about it – and for years, as a consequence of that misunderstanding, I was horrible to her.

Blaming Mum for the separation made me angry enough. But about two years later I was in bed one night when a man's voice in the living room woke me up. I sat bolt upright. Who the hell was that? Flinging off the bed covers, I marched out of my room and burst in on them.

'What's this?' I demanded, glowering at my mum with this strange man. He was Afro-Caribbean and would have been in his thirties, with a round, kind face.

'Go to bed,' she snapped.

'No. Who's this?'

The man said nothing, but looked at Mum.

'What are you doing here?' I shouted at him. 'Get out.' Still he said nothing. 'You'd better get out,' I repeated, and turned to my mum, incredulous. 'I'll ring my dad.'

I knew how frightening he could be. And he was. 'Don't

bring no man to my house when my kids are there!' he used to yell, as he'd blast round at night to try to catch them together. As I look back now, it was madness. The man's name was Peter, and for the first two years of their relation-ship I treated him like dirt.

This would be a typical scene in our flat. I come in from school, in a good mood – and there's Peter on the sofa, watching TV. That's the end of my good mood. I march into the living room, snatch the remote control from him and turn the TV over. I glare at the screen. Peter tries to say something perfectly harmless and friendly – 'How was school today?' My eyes narrow, but remain locked on the screen.

'Don't even chat to me. What you chatting to me for? You don't know me. You're not my dad.'

My mum's sister-in-law was a social worker, and came round to try to work out why I was behaving like a lunatic.

'Because she should be with my dad!' I screamed at her, beside myself. To my mum, I raged, 'It's all cos of you that my dad doesn't live with us any more!' In my confused, hormonal, angry mind, the only obstacle keeping my parents apart was Peter.

I kept up the ferocious hostility for ages. How Peter put up with it I do not know. He was a painter and decorator by trade, but also a deacon in a born-again Christian church, and I must have sorely tested the poor man's capacity to turn the other cheek. But then one day my dad introduced me to his new partner, Lisa, and suddenly – I don't know why – I made peace with the situation, and stopped being furious about it.

Me, Mum with Sian, Peter and Anton

My mum and Peter have been together now for twenty-eight years. He has been an absolute rock for her, and made her very happy. My angry twelve-year-old self had been completely wrong about him. They have had a daughter and a son, and Dad and Lisa – who have been together almost as long – have three girls. To me they are all my brothers and sisters, and I couldn't love them more. Mum and Dad got along well in the end, and with each other's partners; I've known enough divorced parents to realise how rare this can be, and count myself very lucky.

But throughout my childhood, all I wanted was my dad's attention. His praise was all I cared about. At primary school I showed real promise as a gymnast, and was also scouted by the Central School of Ballet and awarded a scholarship. Four nights a week, for four years, after school I would get buses and trains north across the river to the ballet school in Farringdon. I was getting out of Peckham for the first time in my life, meeting people who weren't from our estate, and I loved it. But at twelve I was also showing serious promise on the football pitch, and one evening my dad took me aside.

With two of my sisters, Anya and Chloe, and Dad

'You've got to decide what you want to do, Rio, because you can't do it all. If you're going to start playing football properly and get scouted by a team, the gymnastics and ballet have got to go.' My dad wasn't interested in football. Kung fu was his thing. But I would have done anything to please him – and when he said he would start training my football team, the decision was made. Ballet was over for me, and gymnastics went out of the window too. Football became everything.

At twelve I was playing for a local youth team, Bloomfield Athletic. On Saturday mornings my dad trained the whole team, not in football but in physical exercise. He was phenomenally fit, and had us doing press ups, sit-ups, sprints – and then he would get on his bike and make me run through the streets following him. He'd bring a tennis racket and make me play against the wall – anything to make me stronger, fitter. He made everything a competition, and I was desperate to beat him. He never let me win at anything, not even cards.

I would have done anything to impress him. After a game, my first words as I came off the field were always 'Dad, how did I do?' In the car home I would keep pestering him: 'I was all right, wasn't I?'

He wouldn't even take his eyes off the road. 'Yeah, you were all right.'

I'd sit beside him, thinking, What the fuck have I got to do to please this guy?' If I scored a hat-trick the other dads were all over me: 'Well done, son! That was the sickest hat-trick.' I would smile, but inside all I was thinking was: I don't really care what you think. I want to know what my dad's going to say.

I should have known I was wasting my time. Even when I won the Champions' League at Manchester United, all I got from Dad was a handshake and 'Yes.' People think Sir Alex Ferguson was difficult to please. They should meet my dad.

If you were to ask my dad now, he would say he took after his own father more than he wanted to or liked to admit at that time. Dad spent so much of his younger life trying to be nothing like his dad – but family legacy is a powerful thing. Back then, in his mind, needing praise was a form of weakness, and one he didn't want to indulge. As for un-deserved praise, well, to my dad that was the worst thing anyone could ever give a child. Hearing a coach or other parents tell a boy he had played well, when in my dad's mind he hadn't, used to drive him mad. 'Don't listen to them,' he would say. 'What interest do they have in whether or not you become a good footballer? They don't care.'

By my mid-teens football had become an all-consuming obsession. I was popular at school, and used to have a laugh in class with my mates, but I got into trouble all the time because, for the life of me, I couldn't see the point of what we were studying. With teachers I became increasingly argu-mentative.

'How the hell is algebra going to help me? When am I ever going to use RE in my life? What's that going to do for me? This is just a waste of my time, man.'

In my final year of school, Dad took matters in hand. 'It's very simple, Rio. If you want to carry on playing football, you have to get five GCSEs. You don't get five GCSEs, I'm telling you straight – that'll be the end of football. You'll have to go to college.'

I have never worked so hard in my life. I knew my dad wasn't joking. On my eleventh birthday I had woken up to find my dad had bought me a Labrador puppy. I couldn't believe it. But that very same day, I was suspended over something silly at school. When I got home my dad beat me with a belt, and the next day the puppy was gone.

Despite how hard he could be, I did always know my dad loved me. When I was older, he told me he'd considered moving back to St Lucia after splitting up with my mum, but couldn't bear to be far away from his boys. The better I got at football, the more of his time he spent ferrying me all over London to play, so there was no doubt in my mind about what I meant to him. But there was never any affection or conversation with my dad. I never knew what he was thinking or feeling – and long before I had even left school, that is exactly what people began to say about me.

Since having three daughters with his partner, Dad has softened almost unrecognisably from the father I knew as a child. I have seen my sisters actually *roll their eyes* at him – and get away with it! He loves being a grandfather too, and my children get on brilliantly with him. If my old friends from the estate didn't still joke about the fear he used to strike in us, I might almost start to wonder if I had imagined it. And as I've grown up, whenever I've needed him, he's been there in my life – standing proud and purposeful, with his incredible quiet strength.

I can't remember when my mum began to tell me she loved me. She certainly didn't when I was a child, but somehow over the years she has learned to. She remains fiercely private, though, and a world expert at keeping her business secret. But, then, she had to grow up without a mother, and my dad had to make his way in the world without much love from his father. Neither of them learned to show love in the way most people nowadays would take for granted, and I have come to understand that none of us can give what we have never received. I think Dad would say he has been a much better father than his was, and that is certainly true. Every family tries to improve itself with each new generation, and mine is no different. To this day, though, Dad is still not one for unnecessary conversation.

A year or so ago I went to his gym with him. It has been

With Dad

his gym for as long as I can remember. We were in the sauna when an elderly man, an old friend of his, came in.

'You all right?' My dad nodded to him. I could sense the man staring, eyes widening. My dad carried on talking to me, but after a few minutes the man could no longer keep quiet.

'Julian, is that Rio Ferdinand?'

Dad barely glanced at him. 'Yes.'

'Julian.' His friend was open-mouthed. 'I've known you about . . . I mean, God, how many years have I known you?'

Still my dad barely turned his head. 'Ye-es?'

'And all these years, you never tell me you know Rio Ferdinand?'

I looked at him and grinned. 'He's my dad.'

The poor man was speechless for a moment or two. 'Fuck off,' he spluttered, 'Julian, you've known me all these years – and you never told me he was your son! What's going on?'

My dad shrugged. 'What would I tell you for? I'm not going to come out and just say it.'

CHAPTER FOUR

Learning to Win

IT IS 2002, and I am twenty-four years old. Football is all I care about, all I think about, all I dream about. It's what I live for. And now here I am at Old Trafford, signing for the biggest club in the world. The world's greatest football manager has just paid £30 million for me, the highest transfer fee in British history at the time, making me the most expensive defender on the planet. My mum, dad and Rebecca are with me; the world's press is waiting outside. Does life get much better than this? I don't think so.

But when I leave the room after signing my contract, Sir Alex Ferguson turns to his assistant and asks, 'Is he actually happy about this or not? Cos he sure as hell doesn't look it. Does this lad even want to be here?'

'Oh, don't worry about that,' my mum has to reassure a bemused Sir Alex. 'That's just Rio. He doesn't show emotion.'

Now fast forward six years. Life does get even better. It's the summer of 2008, and I am standing on the pitch of the Luzhniki stadium in Moscow. It's the Champions League Final. I'm the captain, the game has gone to extra time, then a penalty shoot-out – and we've just won. We are European champions.

It is, and will always remain, the single greatest achievement of my sporting career. I lift the cup and the stadium goes wild. Tens of millions of fans are watching on television. Back in the dressing room, I approach the manager and club chairman – and this is what I say: 'Who we buying? Who we buying next year? We've got to get somebody. We need some players. We need to make sure we keep going now. We can win this again next year.'

Sir Alex looks at me as if I've lost my mind. Other players are in each other's arms, whooping and laughing. Champagne bottles are popping – the dressing room is a riot of foaming

As captain, lifting the Champions League Trophy in 2008 with Ryan Giggs

Moët, dancing delirium and unbridled joy. 'Rio,' Sir Alex laughs, 'for fuck's sake, enjoy the party, man.'

I don't even smile back. 'I can enjoy it when you tell me that we're going to get more players, please.'

I'm not just cold by normal people's standards. I'm not just cold by professional footballers' standards. I am cold by the standards of *Sir Alex Ferguson*.

EVEN IF I had never kicked a ball, and had instead become a bus driver, say, it's pretty clear I would always have been a closed book. Growing up in my family, as by now you'll understand, I learned to keep my emotions to myself. But becoming a footballer took this to a completely different level, and made me into something more like a machine than a man. As a professional sportsman you don't just learn to hide your feelings. You learn not to have them.

From the age of twelve, when I began to take football seriously, only one emotion became acceptable to me: hatred of losing. In my childhood on the estate I witnessed all manner of violence and madness, but none of it affected me. Only one thing could ever make me cry – and that was losing.

If I lost at any game of anything at all – not just football but tennis, bike races, cards, literally anything – I would scream and shout and cry like a baby. I am a notoriously terrible loser. After losing to Chelsea at Stamford Bridge in 2008, I was so beside myself that on my way off the field into the tunnel I took a great swing at the wall with my foot – and accidentally kicked a security guard. Even with

Sir Alex, I couldn't always contain my fury in the face of a defeat. We were 1–0 up away against Bayern Munich during a 2010 Champions League match when the boss switched tactics, and we lost 2–1. I was incandescent, and let everyone know. In the dressing room afterwards, he went berserk, screaming at me for undermining him in public.

'I don't care!' I screamed back. 'I want to win, and you fucking made us lose! It's a joke.'

My teammate Gary Neville grabbed my arm. 'Rio, stop, you're not going to win this argument.'

I turned on him. 'Fuck off!'

On the plane home I was still consumed by anguish. I turned to Nemanja Vidić, sitting just across the aisle. 'Vid, you know I'm right, don't you?' It was killing me that the other players felt the same way, yet wouldn't speak their mind to the boss.

'But, Rio,' he pointed out, not unreasonably, 'that's not the point. The point is, you don't argue.'

'But I can't be like that, man. It's not personal. I'm not trying to make myself feel better or look better. It's just purely about – I want the team to win. I'm just desperate – *desperate* – to win.' I genuinely could not control myself.

My former Man United teammate Michael Carrick held a testimonial match recently to mark his retirement, and made little videos about each of his old teammates. Ryan Giggs, for example, was 'player legend'. But me? 'Rio Ferdinand: worst loser *ever.*' I had to laugh. I could hardly disagree. Carrick wasn't wrong.

I've been this way ever since I was a boy. I can't have been more than eleven when my youth team lost a five-a-side tournament match I felt we should have won. I blamed our goalie, and after the final whistle I turned on the poor kid and let rip.

'You're rubbish! You can't do it! Get out. Don't play for us no more. You're going to make us lose. You're rubbish and I never want to see you again. You let us down – you don't want to play, what are you doing on our team? Go home. Don't come on our team again.'

In the car home afterwards even my dad looked slightly shaken by my outburst. 'Rio, I don't ever want to see or hear anything like ever again. Do you understand me?'

Can you imagine what it would take for my *dad* to think I'd gone too far? But still I couldn't promise it wouldn't happen again. It almost certainly would. I cannot stand to lose. It's as simple as that.

It was around this time that my mate Gavin, who was also fanatical about football, told me about a group of guys who played every weekend in Burgess Park, a bike ride away from the estate. These weren't kids but grown men – thirty or so of them, mostly African – and the first week we showed up they didn't even notice us. The park lay just beside a Travellers' camp, and I'd had to force myself to walk past packs of savage dogs, ignoring the catcalls of kids from the camp, just to sit on the grass and be ignored by a bunch of big men who had no time or use for a pair of skinny lads. The following weekend we went back, and the next, and the next – until eventually one week they were short, and the call we had been hoping for came.

'Oi, kid! Want to play some football?'

I'd never played a game like it before. It was not just that they were good – though they were. They were harder and stronger than anyone I had ever played against, and God help you if you held onto the ball. I made that mistake within the very first minute – and was clattered to the ground by a man three times my size. Winded, with a mouth full of grass, I wanted to cry. Then I was back on my feet, pacing, pointing, yelling, 'Gimme the ball again!'

It was an important early lesson in what it takes to push yourself beyond your limits. To feel fear on that pitch, let alone show it, would have spelled the end for me. I had to prove myself tougher than any of them – and one week, as I was leaving the field, came the sweetest words I had ever heard: 'Hey, he's all right him, isn't he? He can play.' I biked home that day feeling like a king. Even at that early age, I understood the significance of what was changing. To be the best, you can't allow yourself the luxury of normal emotions. You don't get to become a winner by being an ordinary boy.

There has been only one time in my life when typical temptations got the better of me, and for a brief while fun came before football. In my late teens, my world underwent the surreal transformation that anyone who has ever found themselves suddenly successful, rich or famous will recognise. One minute I was a mixed-race lad from a Peckham council estate, being turned away from West End designer stores by security guards who took one look and saw nothing but trouble. The next, I was West Ham's hot young defender, with my face all over the papers and my name on the lips of every TV pundit, tipped as a future England star. I was on every guest list in London, party invitations poured in every day, and overnight the city I'd grown up in became my private sweet shop.

Until you undergo this sort of bizarre alchemy, you cannot begin to imagine what it does to you. I lost my head. I bought myself a flat in Wapping, but was still basically living at my mum's, though in truth I was hardly ever home. I'd be out drinking and raving on a Saturday night till six a.m., and back in the pub again by noon on Sunday for another session that could last until four or five the following morning. I'd train on Monday, but by Tuesday night there was always another party invitation, and Wednesday was one of the best club nights in London, so naturally I would be out again. On Thursday night I would manage to stop myself drinking, but still go out. Friday night before a match was about the only night you could rely on me to stay at home. Come Saturday afternoon, after the game, I couldn't get out of the dressing room and back to the bright lights fast enough.

It's a measure of how young and deluded I was that for a brief heady time I actually imagined I could have it all. Reality came as a cold sharp shock, and the price I had to pay still burns me to this day. When the England squad for Euro 2000 was announced, my name wasn't on it. Kevin Keegan and his staff had taken a long, hard look at me, and did not see a man serious about winning. They were right. Of course they were right. But I made sure from that day on that no one would ever think that about me again.

In spite of all my partying, I was still attracting interest from major Premier League clubs, and in particular Chelsea.

Leaving West Ham for Stamford Bridge would have been the easy, obvious choice. But if I stayed in the capital, I would be in a city that threatened to compete with football for my attention – and no way was I going to let that happen again. Leeds might have been a less glamorous option than Chelsea, but that's exactly why I took it. Never again would I let anything but football dictate my life.

The professionalism I found at Leeds confirmed I had made the right decision. The partying calmed down, my focus was back, and two years later I was ready to sign for the most disciplined, dedicated club in world football. At Man United you don't 'play' the game. You are an elite winning machine.

THERE IS A widely held and fundamental misunderstanding that professional sportspeople want to win because it feels good. People always say to me, 'Rio, you must have loved it when you beat so-and-so' – and, yes, to an extent that's true. On the pitch, it's a wicked feeling. But by the time you're back in the dressing room, it has already dulled into relief. The only thought I will allow myself after a win is: Right, job done. Now, when's the next one?

You learn to force yourself down from the adrenalin rush of victory, and flatten your spirits. That game you just won? That game is dead. No matter how well you played, even if you scored ten goals, that game is dead. Within literally minutes I'm no longer enjoying the moment, because the game is already gone. As far as I'm concerned, I didn't even play it. You cannot allow yourself the luxury of satisfaction, because every second spent savouring a victory is a minute wasted that should have been devoted to focusing on the next match. A friend of mine read my 2006 autobiography recently, and couldn't understand why it made so little mention of my success and so much of my losses. If he didn't know better, he joked, he would have been forgiven for thinking my career had been one giant failure.

Winning brings me no joy. All it delivers is relief: relief that I didn't lose. The pleasure of victory is as nothing compared to the pain of defeat, so when I win I'm just relieved I haven't lost and can move on to the next challenge. When I lose, it honestly feels like the end of the world.

I'm not even sure that words exist to convey the depth of horror I feel about losing. It is a toxic fog of humiliation, shame and paranoia. I feel stripped of my dignity and self-respect, crushed; it feels intensely personal. To be out in public is excruciating: I feel as if everyone is staring at me, laughing at me. I scowl at strangers I pass on the street and think, Well, you're obviously a Man City fan. You think you can laugh at me cos we lost, well fuck off. Even on the school run, after a defeat I'd wear a hoodie pulled up. I would have gladly worn a balaclava too it I could.

Even in training, to lose is agony. In the changing room afterwards, your teammates will mock and scorn and jeer – and God knows I'm the worst offender if I win. 'We battered you,' I'll taunt with glee. 'You're shit. Your team are shit. Don't even talk to me. You can't speak to me for the rest of the day. Shut up, you're shit.' I'm just as hard on myself when I lose. 'You are absolutely shit,' I'd tell myself, swallowed up in self-loathing. 'You are a disgrace.'

The darkness lasts for days and days and days. It is beyond my control, like a physical pain. I can't sleep, and when eventually I do, the moment I wake up I'm plunged straight back into the torment. No defeat can be compartmentalised in my mind, or rationalised away, because my entire existence is dedicated to one goal, winning medals, and every match I lose takes me further away from my next medal. People think it must be brilliant to get paid to play football. They don't see the obsessive, all-consuming, relentless rollercoaster of mental and physical preparation and recovery that fills every waking moment of a sportsman's life.

People also think football clubs are close, tight-knit outfits, but again this is wide of the mark. You are not really friends with your teammates: you're just colleagues, united by the common goal to win. The day a player leaves your club, he ceases to exist for you. I invited only two footballers to my wedding – the Chelsea players Jody Morris and Michael Duberry. Of my former Man United teammates, I have remained close to only a handful, and I think most professional footballers would say much the same thing. You're not there to be best friends: you're there to win. Once a player is no longer part of the team, life quickly moves on.

Besides, it's very hard to get close to people if you despise anyone for showing any sign of weakness. If a teammate looks down or, worse still, sorry for himself, you don't feel

sympathy for him. You think: Do not fuck my shit up. I'm
here for one reason – to win – and I'm trying all I can to
achieve it, so you'd better be on the same level. It would
never even enter my head to say: 'You all right, mate? Let's
go and get a coffee.' I'd be thinking, I don't even want to be
in the same room as you. You're weak, man, you're a disgrace.
Because you can't have someone like that in the dressing
room. If I see any sign of weakness, I make a snap judgement: that guy's bad news, he doesn't work hard enough,
he's flaky, his work ethic's non-existent. I have no respect
for him. I want him out, I want him gone. If a player looks
like he could cost me a win, I detest him. It is an intensely
macho culture – and a small world. A player cannot afford
to be seen looking weak many times before word gets around
and his reputation is finished.

Even worse was if a teammate looked as if he didn't mind
losing. I could no more contemplate going out socialising
after losing a match than I could cut my own legs off. In
the early days, if a team mate went out drinking or clubbing,
or even just for dinner, after we lost, I loathed him with a
brutal passion. To me it meant he was only a footballer for
the money: he didn't care about the sport itself, and for that
I detested him. I do not consider the term 'good loser' a
compliment.

What I'm trying to explain is that ordinary human intimacy – the normal stuff of friendship, camaraderie, compassion, forgiveness – does not figure in the mind of a top
sportsman. No relationship matters more than winning.
When I was fifteen I became very close friends with the
future Chelsea captain Frank Lampard. We were both at

West Ham, we were both new young stars and from the age of fifteen to twenty-two we were as close as brothers. We trained together, played together, drank together, holidayed together. I spent most of my formative years with Frank. We were side by side as we grew from boys to men. Then Frank signed for Chelsea, I signed for Man United, and just like that we were practically dead to each other. He was a mortal rival, and from that point on I would have little to do with him. You could say that's a terrible shame – and I can see that in one sense it is – but, honestly, I didn't care. I didn't feel conflicted about the choice I had to make. It was easy. Football would always come before friendship, so what was there to even think about?

Me and Frank Lampard playing for England

Football was not just the most important thing in my life, it was the only thing. Soon after signing for Man United I gave up drinking altogether during the season. I wouldn't go to family social functions, I missed Rebecca's grand-mother's funeral – I even missed my daughter Tia's birth. I was down in London with Man United playing in a cup semi-final when Rebecca went into labour in Manchester. By the time I could get north to the hospital, Tia was already born.

Most people live their lives with all sorts of competing priorities. Life is a balancing act, I hear people say. But for a footballer there are no dilemmas and there is no balance, because the only criterion for every choice you ever make is: will this make me a better player? Your club makes sure of this by taking care of every single tiny detail of your life, so that you have just one thing to focus on: being the best.

You do not lift a finger until you step over that white line onto the pitch to play football. In the dressing room, you find your kit prepared and waiting in your locker. After the game you throw it on the floor, like a toddler getting changed. When your boots are muddy, someone takes them away, cleans them and returns them to your hand. You live like a medieval lord, surrounded by courtiers and servants. I have travelled all over the world in my career, but until the day I retired I'd never once in my life had to look up at an airport departures board or gate sign. You lounge about with the team, and when it's time to move you just follow feet. You don't even look up.

Until the moment you step onto the field, every dimension of your existence is taken care of. Each club has a player liaison officer, whose job is to look after your every need. From the moment I signed for West Ham, I didn't have to concern myself with any of the ordinary milestones of adult-hood. Want to buy a house? Insure a car? See a dentist? Fill out a tax form? Someone else does it for you. Your club wraps you up in cotton wool, to the extent – and I know this sounds truly bizarre – that I was not even allowed to cut my own toenails. A club staff member had to do it for me, to make sure my feet didn't get hurt.

By now I hope you understand me when I say that elite sportsmen are not normal people. We do not develop into grounded, well-rounded three-dimensional adults because nothing about our psyche or our lifestyle is designed for normal life. In the gym you often see blokes who work on just one area of their body, to the exclusion of everything else: they will have skinny little legs but great bulging biceps or a barrel of a chest. Being a professional sportsman is a bit like that. We develop just one muscle – the ability to win – and neglect every other aspect of ourselves. I have won a lot of runners-up medals in my career, and couldn't even tell you where they are. They mean less than nothing to me.

Only once in my adult career did I lower my guard and allow myself to feel an ordinary emotion. It was at the 2002 World Cup finals in Japan. We were drawn against Brazil in the quarter-finals, and as the teams lined up before the match I looked over at legend after legend – Ronaldo, Rivaldo, Ronaldinho. Mum and Dad were in the crowd, so was Rebecca, and when the national anthem began to play something inside me cracked. Right there, right then, I had everything I'd ever dreamed of. And I wept.

I played appallingly. I'd lost my focus. We were beaten 2–1. And I never, ever let it happen again.

When life was good I don't think I gave a thought to the

price I might one day pay for the strange asymmetry of my sportsman's mindset. I never stopped to wonder how I would cope in a situation that was not about winning. It didn't even occur to me that one day I would need muscles I had never developed.

CHAPTER FIVE

Fame and Fortune

I'M TWENTY YEARS old. I'm still living in London, playing for West Ham and loving the nightlife. One of the best nights in town is Saturday night at the Emporium club. It's a Premier-League-footballers-and-models sort of scene, with wall-to-wall Bollinger and Gucci, and paparazzi at every exit. But the music is amazing, the VIP bar is a riot and, needless to say, I'm there most weeks.

This is what I see when I walk in. Glossy blondes are perching on bar stools; foxy brunettes drape themselves around tables near the dance floor. Pneumatic beauties are spilling out of barely there mini-dresses whichever way I turn. Quite a few of them clock me when I walk in. And – with varying degrees of subtlety – they make their move.

It sounds like every young guy's dream, doesn't it? Only it's not. That girl over there by the door? She's a kiss-and-tell specialist. Her near the bar? She's another. That one talking to a QPR youth team player? Her game plan is to get herself pregnant. The one ordering cocktails? She's actually looking for a footballer to settle down with. Hmm, good luck with that.

If this makes me sound cynical, that's because I am. I know that most of these girls wouldn't look twice at me if I was a plumber and still lived on a Peckham council estate. I'm not stupid. Their smiles are as fake as their fluttering eyelashes, and behind their come-to-bed eyes these women are counting and calculating. When they gaze into mine, all they see are pound signs.

YOU ALREADY KNOW what the culture of football and my family background had done to my ability to be open or intimate. Now, can you imagine what this kind of fame and wealth did for my trust issues – whether or not this was really true?

When it came to girls, I was cagey long before riches and fame complicated the matter even further. I won't say I always got it right on the kiss-and-tell front but for a lot of boys when I was growing up, having a girlfriend was the be-all and end-all of everything. It was never that way for me. For me, having a girlfriend meant letting someone know my business, and even as a child I couldn't stand having to answer to anybody. Getting a girlfriend wasn't what would complete me, and I never felt as if I had to prove myself in that way. The only place I needed to prove myself was on the pitch.

There is an old joke that always makes me laugh. A man gets washed up on a desert island, and the only other survivor of the shipwreck is Halle Berry. The two hit it off, and within a week they're sleeping together. Each night their sex life gets wilder and wilder, until one night Halle looks at him as they lie under the stars, and she says, 'Tell me what you want. What is your craziest, deepest desire? Tell me, and I'll do it. I will do literally anything you want.'

'Seriously?' the guy says. 'You really mean it? Wow.' He thinks for a moment, while she gazes at him, wondering what his deepest, darkest fantasy will be. 'Okay,' he says. 'Will you do this for me? Will you let me draw a moustache on your face?'

'Er, okay,' she says, slightly surprised.

'And then,' he goes on, 'will you let me call you Simon? That's my best mate's name.'

'Er . . . okay. If that's what you really, really want.'

'It is,' he says. So he draws a moustache on her face, and tells her to go and stand under a palm tree and wait. Seconds later he runs up, grabs her by the shoulder, spins her round and yells: 'Simon, Simon, Simon! Mate! You're never gonna believe who I'm shagging. I'm shagging Halle Berry!'

This joke makes me laugh because I know how true it is for most men. It just never was for me. At school I once dumped a girl because she told a few people she was going out with me. I never wanted anyone to think they could go about saying, 'I'm Rio's girlfriend.' I realise that probably makes me sound arrogant – but to me it just felt perfectly simple.

It was largely because of this that I didn't bring girls home to meet my mum. Obviously I knew that was what most of my mates were doing, but I couldn't think of anything worse, and privately thought it was disgraceful of them. I couldn't bear the idea of Mum seeing girls coming in one door and out the other, so out of respect to her – and in a way, I guess, to them – I made sure that did not happen. To meet my mum would signify a girl's importance to me, and until I met a girl I felt that way about, I didn't want anyone to get the wrong idea.

I did bring one girl home to my mum's flat, when I was seventeen – but only because I was certain Mum, Peter, my brothers and sister were all going to be out. I will never forget the panic of hearing a key in the lock and my mum's footsteps in the hall. I froze.

'Listen,' I hissed. 'Shut up, don't you dare speak – you stay here, understand? Do. Not. Move.'

I left the girl hiding under the bed while I went downstairs and managed to get Mum out of the flat under some pretext or other, then dashed back indoors and bundled the poor girl out.

My scepticism about girlfriends had a lot to do with the fact that they always seemed to want to talk about feelings. 'This is how I feel about you, blah-blah. How do you feel about me?' It drove me mad. I used to think, Why are you going on about feelings? What's that got to do with anything? To me it was invasive, and uncomfortable. I didn't want to get close to a girl: that sort of emotional intimacy held no value to me. I just wanted to meet up, fool around and chip off – 'See you later.' I didn't want any chat, because it was not something I had ever been used to. I know this sounds raw, but we are all a product of our upbringing, and that's just the way I always was.

But when you find yourself earning millions of pounds,

suddenly every girl you meet seems to want to say, 'I'm Rio's girlfriend.' Wealth makes you intensely suspicious of motives, and wary of every woman you meet. Plainly it would be grotesque to complain about earning millions, and please don't get me wrong: I've been grateful for every penny I've earned. But to say that wealth doesn't come with a price tag would be naïve.

I've always loved nice things, so it was thrilling to join West Ham and suddenly be able to buy them. If I'm honest, I got a bit carried away with myself. I remember standing on the balcony of my mum's flat, looking down at the brand new BMW convertible I had just bought myself. Dad was standing beside me, and I could have burst with pride and

With Mum and one of my Premier League medals

excitement. 'Look at it, Dad. Look at my car. What do you think?'

'Yeah,' he said quietly. 'And your mum's still living in a council flat.'

'Oh.' That was all I think I said. 'Oh.' But his words winded me, like a punch to the stomach. What had I been thinking? I could have died of shame. The very next thing I bought was a house for my mum.

With close family, wealth solves problems. With everyone else, however, it creates complications. I don't know whether you would laugh or cry if I told you how much money I've given people over the years, but the brutal truth is that money destroys the purity of relationships. People begin to question you if you don't give them things – and in turn you begin to question them when you do. Do they want to be my mates because they genuinely like me – or because of what I can buy them? The bitter irony is that I have given far more financial help to the people in my life who aren't even my closest friends. My oldest mates from Peckham are getting by on so much less, yet they are not the ones who ask for anything.

Even if people aren't interested in your money, you always wonder if your fame is the main appeal for them. Since the age of about eighteen, every time I meet someone I have to work out if they're pleased to meet me for myself or because I'm 'Rio Ferdinand'. I soon learned how to spot the latter, because most men can't hide it. Straight off they start talking to me about football, asking, 'What's this player like?' and 'What's that one like?' I think, I'm not here to gossip about my teammates. I don't even know you. Why are you asking me all these stupid questions?

Everyone always likes to think this wouldn't be the case for them, if they were to become rich and famous – but, trust me, it would. As a consequence, you find it extremely difficult to trust people. Other than the friendships I've made in professional football, I don't think I've made many true new friends since I was about sixteen.

Trying to mix mates from my old life with people from my new one wasn't always plain sailing. Early on in my career I went away on holiday with four or five of my childhood friends, plus some footballers and a few of theirs. I practically had to stop my guys from robbing them. I had to sit them down and give them a serious talking to. 'Listen, you're with me. You can't do that mad kind of shit.'

But my guys had only ever lived by the code of life on the estate and, as far as they were concerned, the usual rules applied. These new guys weren't from their estate – so in their eyes, they were fair game.

I soon discovered that I was fair game, too, in the eyes of all the 'financial advisers' and interior designers and lawyers and agents and salesmen and other liberty-takers who flock round a young footballer, like moths to a flame. They see an unworldly young kid earning big cash, and they will do anything to ingratiate themselves and manipulate him for profit. And in one sense, who could blame them? It's easy pickings. In the early days of my career, my life was moving so fast, and there was so much to think about, that when a plausible-sounding fellow offered to get me a state-of-the-art new car, was I going to say no? Two years later I would look more closely and realise I'd paid £105,000 for an £80,000 car. But, of course, you don't look at the small print when you're signing on the dotted line: you just want to get the car on the road. When you have money coming out of your ears, you can spend £25,000 over the odds and afford not to notice.

Like all Premier League footballers, as I grew older I quickly wised up. I was not a sitting duck for long. But the legacy of being exploited never leaves you, and for me it only compounded my instinctive wariness. The press, of course, made matters even worse. I hadn't been at West Ham long when I gave my first big in-depth interview to a journalist. She said she wanted to do a 'lifestyle' interview, to help the public get to know me – and, like a fool, I spoke freely. She twisted every single word I said, and annihilated me.

In recent years I have tried to communicate directly with the public. I have more than twenty million followers on social media, and to be able to connect with fans without relying on intermediaries has been life-changing for me. I love it. But social media comes with its own complications, and there is so much ugly trolling online that you have to develop an armour-plated skin. Once again, that involves shutting down your emotions.

I learned my lesson the hard way from that first press interview, and was always militantly guarded in media interviews from then on. But the thing about fame is that it takes on a life of its own, beyond your control. By the time I signed for Man United, it had become pretty much impossible for me to do normal everyday things, like go shopping or see a movie. A baseball cap with the brim worn low became my uniform – and, I guess, a symbol of my relationship with the world. I even stopped going to family functions. My mum became so protective of me that she wouldn't even let relatives in the wider family have my phone number. 'Come through me,' she'd tell them. 'If you want to talk to Rio, you go through me.'

Looking back now, I can see it was a kind of perfect storm. Every single formative experience in my life reinforced the same message. Do not trust anyone. Do not lower your guard. Do not let anyone come close. Do not open up.

That, in a nutshell, is the person I was when I met Rebecca. To a greater or lesser extent, it's the person I remained until the day she died.

CHAPTER SIX

Finding the One

IT IS SATURDAY night, around midnight, in the early summer of 2000. I'm out. Of course I'm out. My favourite venue at this time is a place called Titanic, but tonight we're at Sugar Reef, another bar nearby in the West End. I'm with a couple of other young West Ham players, and some of my old friends from the estate in Peckham. We're drinking near the bar, having a laugh, when I glance across and spot a girl I know.

She's from Essex. I don't know her very well, but my mate Frank Lampard does. He isn't out with us tonight, though. I probably wouldn't have bothered going over to say hello, except that when I glance again, I notice the girl next to her. She has long, glossy dark hair, piercing green feline eyes, sparkling skin and an hourglass knockout figure. Something inside me switches on.

'All right, what's happening?' I grin, sidling up to the girl I vaguely know. 'Having a good night? Who's that you're with?'

She gives me one of those weary, don't-even-think-about-it looks.

'Sort me out with your mate,' I persist.

'No. She won't go out with you. She won't go out with footballers.'

'All right.' I grin again. But I have no intention of walking away.

Her friend is wearing a top with a strap down the centre of her back. I reach across and snap it with a finger. I know, I know. Not exactly classy or subtle. She spins around. 'What are you doing?'

'Oh, nothing.'

We start to talk.

It's going quite well. After a few minutes, I deliver what I'm sorry to say was one of my stock lines at the time. 'Listen. Go to the bar, get a pen and paper, write your number down and bring it back to me.'

She looks at me as if I must be out of my mind. 'No. I won't be doing that.'

What? This isn't what normally happens. Does she mean it? Shit, I think she actually does.

A little while later I'm dancing when I glance over again and, damn it, my mate's talking to her. He's a bit of a lunatic, this friend. We don't know it now, but by the end of the summer he'll be in prison. I make my way over and join them. 'What's going on here, then?'

'Oh,' she says, coolly. 'I'm just telling him that you're giving me your number. We're exchanging numbers.' I look at my friend, trying not to smile.

'Well, you'd better move then, mate. You'd better move.' I take the girl's hand, we go to the bar, I ask for a pen, and write my number on a scrap of paper. She tells me hers, and I scribble it down.

'What's your name?' I ask.

'It's Rebecca.'

When I wake up the following day, what happens next is unprecedented. The first thing I do is find the number and pick up the phone. In my life I have never got a girl's number on a Saturday night and phoned her on Sunday morning. This is not me. I like to play the cool game, but with this girl I can't contain myself. I don't know what it is about her that has got under my skin, but she is all I can think about. I dial the number.

'Hello?' It isn't her. It's her friend from last night.

'Can I speak to Rebecca?'

'Yes, she's here.' She passes the phone over.

'When are we going to meet up then? I'd like to take you out for something to eat.'

There is silence on the line. My heart stops.

'Okay, then. Yes.'

REBECCA WAS THE middle child of an inspector in the Metropolitan Police and a nurse, and grew up in Chingford, Essex, on the outskirts of east London, with her elder sister and younger brother. They were a conventional, close-knit family, but from the earliest age Rebecca was unusually single-minded. On her very first day at nursery, when she was barely more than a toddler, the staff asked her to put an apron on before painting. Rebecca didn't want to wear an apron, and that was that. She never went back to the nursery.

Another family story always makes me smile. At secondary

97

school there was a teacher who had it in for Rebecca's sister. When Rebecca joined the school, he assumed he could bully her too. Rebecca always wore make-up to school, even though it was not allowed, and the teacher summoned her and some other girls wearing offending eyeliner into the toilets. He lined them up side by side in front of the mirror.

'Look at yourselves!' he barked. 'What do you see in the mirror?'

Rebecca did not miss a beat. 'Well, I see the most beautiful girl in the world. What do you see?' He never bothered her again.

Rebecca got along fine at school, but her heart was never there. As a child what she really loved was dance and, like me, she did a lot of ballet. In her teens, again like me, her other passion became fashion, and from an early age she worked part-time jobs so that she could buy herself clothes. In her teens she looked much older than her age, and used to borrow her big sister's ID. Employers never guessed, and even if they had, I doubt it would have made any difference. Rebecca was too much of a charmer and a grafter for anyone to care how old she was.

She used to work at Walthamstow market selling shirts, and would be up at dawn on a Saturday morning, stuffing her shoes with cardboard to keep her feet warm, before catching a bus down to east London. On Sundays she sold bikinis at another market, and whenever other traders were away they would ask her to run their stalls for them. I can see why. Rebecca had the gift of the gab: she could have sold ice to the Eskimos.

She also worked in a local restaurant, and with her sister

at a wine bar called Jets. At one point she, her mum and her sister all worked at the D. H. Evans department store on Oxford Street in London. If she was popular with employers, she was quite the hit with the customers too. On Valentine's Day one year, when she could only have been sixteen, a delivery man from Harrods in a top hat and tails showed up at D. H. Evans with a bouquet of flowers for her from an admirer. It was so tall and wide, she could barely get it home on the tube.

Even from an early age, she had a certain toughness – I think she must have got it from her dad – and she didn't suffer fools gladly. If a sales assistant ignored Rebecca when she was waiting to buy something, she could be very sharp. 'Do you actually work here? Do you? Because you've just lost a sale.' Out of the shop she would stalk. Her mum and sister would be cringing with embarrassment, but Rebecca didn't care.

She was fiercely – and I mean *fiercely* – protective of her family. If someone trod on her mum's toe on the tube, in a flash she would turn on them. 'That is my mother, you know. You have just stood on her foot.' Once, when her brother was visiting, the pair got into an argument, and I made the fatal mistake of trying to intervene. Oh, my God, never again. Rebecca could say what she liked to her family – but good luck to anyone who tried to join in.

After GCSEs she stayed on in the sixth form to study A levels, but a close friend of hers worked for an accounts company in London, and happened to mention one day that they were looking for someone to employ in their banking department. Was Rebecca interested? She went for an interview, and afterwards the boss rang her mum.

'The reason I've given your daughter the job is because by the time she left she knew how much I earned, where I lived, how many children I had and the name of my wife. She interviewed me, not the other way around.' That was the end of school for Rebecca. She bought herself a smart suit and a commuter-train season ticket, and was off to work in London.

Because she looked so much older than her age, Rebecca was already used to going out in London. She was not one for socialising in a big group, but liked to go out with her best friend, her sister and her sister's best friend. Rebecca was the one who would go to the bar to buy the drinks, even though she was the youngest, as she could always get served. If there was ever any trouble while they were out Rebecca would find the nearest police officer and explain who her dad was. The officer would escort them to a nearby police station, call her dad, and he would come and collect them. That probably helps to explain her precocious social confidence; Rebecca was not afraid of anyone or anything.

Weirdly, despite what she said to the teacher that day in the toilets, she did not consider herself a beauty. I don't know why. The firm where she worked had a flat upstairs, and if staff were going out later they could book the flat in advance and use it to get changed and made-up. The first time she put her name down in the book, every man in the office promptly added his name too. She was mortified with embarrassment, but somehow still did not get the message that she was drop-dead gorgeous.

I didn't find this out until much later, but on the morning after I met Rebecca in the bar, she told her mum that she had been asked out by a footballer. Somebody asked her what this footballer was called.

'I think it's Furry-hand,' she said.

'You mean Ferdinand?'

She shrugged. 'Oh, yeah, it might be. He's asked me out to dinner. What do you think?'

Her mum hadn't heard of me either. 'Well, he's not asking you to marry him, is he? So why not? You might as well. It'll be nice.'

Nobody in her family was a big football fan, and Rebecca certainly wasn't. I was the first player she had ever met, and she could not have been less interested in the game. She was quite old-fashioned in a way, very proper and correct – the polar opposite of the kiss-and-tell girls I was used to meeting in West End bars. After agreeing to have dinner with me, she told her mum, 'If he beeps outside when he comes to pick me up, he'll wait there all night. I'm not going out to the car if he beeps. He's got to come and knock on the door.'

Luckily, I did. Her dad answered. 'She's upstairs getting ready. Come in.' I was not really used to meeting parents – let alone a police-officer dad – and the family had two dogs, which didn't help, as I have always been scared of them. I was trying to act cool as I sat down on the sofa to wait, then saw they were watching a programme about the Ku Klux Klan. Was this some kind of a joke? Then I realised it was a *Ruby Wax Meets . . .* documentary, and relaxed. A minute or two later Rebecca appeared, and off we went.

I took her to a restaurant in Kensington called Scalini, a traditional Italian place. I felt strangely relaxed. There were no first-date nerves. When the waiter came Rebecca began to order something vegetarian, then broke off and started to laugh.

'Listen, deep down I actually want to eat the fattest thing on the menu. But I thought you play football so I'd better be healthy.' Ditching the lettuce option, she ordered a starter, main and dessert. I think she was the first girl I had ever taken out who ate all three courses.

Already I knew I liked her. But by that point in my career I had learned to ask certain questions on a first date, to try to establish whether a girl was actually interested in me or in what I did for a living. 'So,' I said to her casually, 'do you work?'

She looked surprised. 'Yes, of course. I work for an accountancy firm.'

Cool. 'Say you met someone who earned a bit of money. Would you want to quit your job?'

She looked even more surprised. 'Are you mad? No, I'd want to keep working.'

Right answer again. She had values, and a work ethic, and although she was beautiful she cared about much more than just superficial appearances. After dropping her home I found myself driving back to London with one thought in my head. I'd never thought it about anyone before, but there was no doubt in my mind now: She's going to be my girl.

I very nearly blew it on our second date. I took her to an absolute dive near the Blackwall Tunnel called Dorringtons. It had a reputation – almost certainly deservedly so – as a bit of a druggie pub, which was not my thing at all, but it played some of the best dance music in London on a Sunday, and music absolutely was my thing. I had a friend with me, and told him to stay with Rebecca while I shot off round the pub talking to people. When I rejoined her ten minutes later, she was deeply unimpressed.

'Don't ever do that again. You just walked off and left me. No, do not do that again.'

The atmosphere in the car as we left Dorringtons was decidedly frosty, but my heart was starting to glow. The honest, if unedifying, truth was that up until that point every girl I had ever taken out had let me get away with murder. 'What do you want to do, Rio? Let's do whatever you want, Rio.' But this girl? She had some bite. She was no pushover, and I really, *really* liked that about her.

I'm not going to pretend this was some sort of fairy-tale romance overnight. In the early weeks I was still running around seeing other girls, and that summer I went away to Ayia Napa in Cyprus for a holiday with Frank Lampard and about half a dozen other footballing friends. I got up to exactly the sort of things you might imagine a young man who still thought of himself as single would do, and this did not strike me as unreasonable. Two weeks later, I was out shopping with my dad when my phone rang. It was a newspaper reporter, calling to inform me that the paper was about to publish a story about me with a young woman in an Ayia Napa hotel room.

But Rebecca was breathtakingly cool about the situation. As she saw it, we had only been out a few times. I was not her boyfriend, and it would be naïve to expect me to behave as if I was.

By the end of that summer we were seeing each other two or three times a week, and beginning to feel more and more like a couple. It seemed incredibly grown-up to me to have a girlfriend, but I liked the feeling. Although I spent most of my time at my mum's house, by then I had bought the flat in Wapping, and it was something of a moment when I made space in the wardrobe for her clothes. We never went out clubbing together. It was always drinks and dinner, then back to the flat. Even though she was not interested in football, I invited her to watch me play for West Ham, and while the game itself meant nothing to her, I sensed she enjoyed seeing me in my world.

All my life I had had a restless, edgy kind of energy. Everything had to happen at a million miles an hour. I could never sit still. But Rebecca made me feel calm, somehow. When I was out and about I was like a wild man – drunk, loud, unstoppable – but as soon as I came into her presence I would sense the adrenalin drain away, and for once would feel at peace. I felt comfortable with Rebecca in a way I had never known before.

Nothing ever felt like an effort with Rebecca. We were never stuck for things to say, and always made each other laugh. Perhaps even more importantly, she liked to laugh at herself. She had two very different sides to her. She could be startlingly cold with strangers in public. She was quick to judge, and if she didn't like you she wasn't going to waste her time being friendly. If someone was behaving like an idiot, she made no bones about it: 'You're a fucking idiot.' But in private she was tender and loving – although she did like to wind people up.

She could say something horribly sharp, just to see the reaction. Jamie, my agent, didn't know what to make of her

With Rebecca

at first because for a joke she would call him up and pretend to complain. 'Why haven't you called that person?' she would demand. 'What? You still haven't spoken to him? Call yourself an agent? I thought you were meant to be an agent! Can't you get this sorted?' I'd hear Jamie stammering something down the line, then watch Rebecca double up laughing. 'Jamie, relax! I'm only messing with you.' I know it's a terrible cliché to say that men marry women just like their mothers, but the truth is she did remind me a lot of my mum.

I think the first time she met my mum it was in the Players' Lounge at West Ham after a game. Mum was ferociously protective of me, and her default position towards any girl was guarded suspicion. But she took to Rebecca immediately, and soon it felt only natural to invite her home to Mum's house so they could meet properly. My mum fell for her exactly as I did.

'She's lovely, Rio.' She smiled approvingly, after Rebecca had gone. 'She's the girl next door, isn't she?'

Mum was right. She was. One of the first things Rebecca said to me when we were getting to know each other was: 'I don't want to be in the papers.' I think she had assumed I must be interested in fame, and would have ideas about setting up paparazzi shots to turn us into some sort of celebrity couple. Nothing could have been further from the truth.

'Don't worry about that,' I reassured her. 'Me neither. I don't want to be in the papers. I'm happy on the back pages – the sports pages – but that's as far as it goes. If I go anywhere with you, we won't arrive together, and we won't leave at the same time. I'm not interested in me or you, let alone us, being in the public eye.'

Before meeting Rebecca I had seen a couple of girls in the entertainment industry, but deep down I think I always knew that that kind of scene was not going to be right for my football career. I made a cold, calculated decision: no way was anyone famous going to become my girlfriend. Remember, this was when David and Victoria Beckham were becoming Posh and Becks – tabloid darlings, king and queen of *OK!* magazine – and I knew that kind of profile was not for me. I did not want to be known as one half of a celebrity couple. I wanted to be known for my football, and nothing else. In my mind, a famous girlfriend could jeopardise my success. Teammates would look at me differently, fans might not take me seriously. Sir Alex Ferguson might not want to buy me.

I valued what privacy I had too much to risk attracting attention with a famous girl on my arm. I would have felt trapped in a celebrity relationship. I wanted the freedom to go for a coffee without a paparazzo's lens trained on my every move.

Going out with a professional sex symbol would have presented another problem. I was so susceptible to intense jealousy. Rebecca was only eighteen when we met, but she carried herself with tremendous self-respect, and that mattered enormously to me. I had no interest in being with a girl who made herself look available to men. I just could not have coped with that: the jealousy would have destroyed me. I hated the sensation, because it made me feel weak, and I would do anything to conceal it, but inside it would make my blood boil. If a girl made me feel jealous, I wanted nothing to do with her.

'This is so unbelievably one-sided,' Rebecca used to say.

And she was right. Whenever I went out I would get a lot of attention from women, and I was well aware that this double standard was a tricky one to justify or defend. My sister Chloe is a proper feminist, and we always argued about this. 'How can you even think like that?' she would say.

Sometimes I asked myself the same question. But my answer was always the one I gave to Chloe: 'It may be sexist – but I don't care. I can't help it.' The thought of my woman giving any man the idea that he might have an opportunity is like mental torture to me. I could never allow myself to be put in that position – and with Rebecca I would never have to.

Given how emotionally guarded I was, this should tell you just how hard I fell for Rebecca. We had only been seeing each other for a few months and were lying in bed one night when I heard the words 'I love you.'

Rebecca had not said them. It was me. Without planning it, or meaning to, or even realising what I'd said until the words were out, I had told her I loved her.

She did not react. She did not say anything. In the darkness I felt my toes curl and face flush. You fucking idiot, I told myself, mortified. What did you go and say that for?

But it was the truth. I did love her. And I always would.

CHAPTER SEVEN

Love and Football

IT IS MID-SEASON, early in 2004. I'm now playing for Manchester United, and for England. It's a Thursday afternoon and I'm home from training. I've had a rest, and come downstairs, and we're standing in the kitchen. Rebecca is saying something to me – but I couldn't tell you what.

'I'm talking,' she says eventually. 'And you're not even listening. You're not even here.'

And she's right. I'm not. I can't even hear what she's saying: my mind is elsewhere. What I'm thinking is: So what am I going to eat? I'm going to have to eat in twenty minutes. I've got a game on Tuesday – I need to get some carbs, carbs, carbs. Where's my pasta?

WHEN I THINK about it now – and I do, a lot – I'm in awe of how Rebecca adjusted to life as the partner of a professional footballer. She was just eighteen, and we had known each other for just six months when she left her family to come to Leeds with me. We loaded up her little Ford Fiesta with her things, and I drove her from Essex to a new life in the north that would have challenged anyone, let alone a teenager. It says everything about her strength of character that she found her feet so fast and made such a success of it.

We lived in Leeds for two years, then moved to a small town just south of Manchester. Rebecca transferred to the Leeds office of her accountancy firm, but when we moved across to Manchester she worked as a personal trainer.

If I'm one of the most disorganised people I know, Rebecca was one of the most organised I've ever met. She was like a force of nature with a pen and a to-do list, and took charge of everything. Both of our families came to visit a lot, and she would take care of all the arrangements. My mind needed to be free for football: I couldn't afford to let it be clogged up with domestic details.

She was intensely house proud, and made a beautiful home for us, always immaculate and full of fresh flowers. Everything from the fridge-freezer to the social calendar was her domain, and I was able to focus on my performance because I knew she had everything under control. What I didn't know for years was that often she would do it all while still in her pyjamas, and fly about the house putting on make-up and getting dressed up just before I got home from training. When I walked through the door every day she looked like a million dollars. I quite literally did not know how lucky I was.

My professional routine dominated our domestic life entirely. When we first moved to Leeds, my mum came to stay in order to essentially give Rebecca a tutorial in my needs. If she couldn't cook, our relationship would not work, and I liked certain Caribbean dishes, like brown stew chicken. Rebecca was impressively pragmatic about it. 'I know that's the type of food you want, so I need to know how to make it.' Mum showed her how to make the meals I liked, and Rebecca became a wicked cook – but the tutorial went way beyond food.

'When he's sleeping, let him sleep,' Mum taught her. After training I had to have precisely two hours' sleep to maximise my body's recovery, and woe betide anyone who disturbed my rest. My agent and best friend, Jamie, could drive all the way up from London – but if he arrived while I was sleeping, even he had to tiptoe in and be as quiet as a mouse until I woke up. Jamie established a rule whereby he wasn't allowed to talk to me about anything but football for forty-eight hours before a match. There were other rules too: I needed to eat complex carbohydrates forty-eight hours before a game, and at other moments it had to be protein. In many ways, living with me was like living with a new-born baby. 'Make sure,' my mum told Rebecca, 'you run everything around making Rio a better footballer. Do not expect or ask him to do anything around the house because for him to become a better footballer – and for you two to have a happy life – he needs his time and headspace free to dedicate to football. Do not be surprised – this is how he is, and how he lives.'

'Your mum is so interfering!' Rebecca protested privately at first – and who could blame her? I don't imagine Mum was always entirely diplomatic. As far as she was concerned, the situation was very straightforward: her son needed this, so this was what his partner had to do.

Printed in black and white on the page, I can see how

strange all of this must seem. But to me it was perfectly normal. We could have planned a weekend visit from friends for weeks, they could have driven all the way up from London and Rebecca could have booked a restaurant table – but if we lost the match that Saturday afternoon, or even if I just played badly, all plans went out of the window. After a bad game I would come home in a black mood with a face like thunder, and sit in front of the television in stony silence until four or five in the morning. The idea that I could go out after a defeat was laughable. Even calling the restaurant to cancel our table was beyond me, and Rebecca knew not to so much as knock on the living-room door with a cup of tea.

I look back now and think, You ignorant bastard. But it was how I needed to be to achieve my best. I didn't even feel guilty for making everyone cancel the plans to go out, any more than I would have felt bad if their plans had been rained off by bad weather. It was just the way it was.

Rebecca and I were not able to spend a single full Christmas Day together. Once we had opened presents and had lunch I was gone, off to the team hotel to get ready for the big Boxing Day game. We were never able to go away for New Year, or take a winter break or go skiing. If I was playing for England in a big summer tournament like the Euros or the World Cup I would get just two weeks off in a year, between the end of the season and the start of pre-season training and foreign-club tours, and for the benefit of team morale I would always go away with my team mates for some of it. And then there were the weekends I needed with my other mates too.

The incredible thing about Rebecca was that she understood. She got it, and sacrificed everything for me. She didn't question it, or try to make me feel guilty about it, and she never, ever complained. She understood me, and what winning meant to me. Rebecca was willing to suspend her own life and sacrifice her own needs to help me be the best.

People think being a WAG offers a woman an enviable lifestyle but, trust me, the reality is nothing like the fantasy they see on *Footballers' Wives.* That lifestyle might be available to girls who go out with the sort of player who is out drinking every night, turning up to the opening of an envelope – the type who will never make it to the elite level. I know, because I used to be that guy – and if I hadn't changed, I very much doubt you would have heard of me. To be the best in the world, you don't just have to be an elite athlete. You have to be an elite thinking athlete. The difference between a player who would be fun to go out with and one like me isn't even the level of Premier League football at which he plays. It is the mental level at which he operates.

Rebecca understood all of this. She knew that if she wanted to come on this journey with me, there would be many lonely nights at home, many holidays on her own with the kids. She knew she would come second, that she would have to think about everything I needed to make me a great footballer before she ever thought about herself. The lifestyle I could offer was not some cute romantic dream. It was tough, and lonely – and the beauty of Rebecca was that she understood all of this, and still loved me enough to say, 'For you, I am willing to do this.'

Her mum said something very insightful recently. She thinks Rebecca was able to sacrifice herself for my career because her father's job as a police inspector had always come first in her own family when she was a child. They were never able to have a Sunday roast together, and at any moment her dad could be called away to deal with an emergency. Rebecca was extremely close to her father, so she knew it was possible to have a solid bond with someone whose work kept taking him away. I don't know how many other women could have made the sacrifices I asked of Rebecca. Had she not grown up with a father whose job always came first, perhaps it would have been too much even for her.

What I admired and loved about Rebecca was her ability to see the bigger picture and play the long game. Footballers' careers are short, and mine would be over long before I reached forty. She had the clarity of mind, and pragmatic self-control, to sacrifice her present for our future together. Rebecca knew there would come a time when I hung up my boots and could devote myself to her and our family. She was willing to wait for me – and for that she earned my deepest respect.

What torments me – it has driven me to the bleakest brink of dark despair – is that I did not get the chance to pay her back. She never got her time.

BECOMING PARENTS DID, of course, change our lives dramatically. We always knew we wanted to have children, but Rebecca was never especially broody or maternal. Even as a child, she didn't like playing with dolls. But she knew she wanted us to have a family of our own.

We waited five years before we felt ready for children, and all three pregnancies were planned, if not exactly fun for Rebecca. She gained four stone during the first, and used to joke that even her ears had got fat. The final weeks of the pregnancy coincided with the World Cup finals in Germany, and she spent a miserable month in a hotel in Baden-Baden, feeling like a whale, while the rest of the WAGS were prancing about in tiny bikinis for the cameras. One afternoon the minibus taking them on an outing dropped them off in the wrong place, and they had to climb a hill on foot. Rebecca literally could not do it. Her legs were swollen and chafing in the heat, and eventually she and her mum had to ask three men passing by for help. One stood either side and took an arm, the third stood behind her and pushed, and together they hauled her up the hill, like removals men shifting a piano.

We were worried that she might go into labour during a match, and arranged for a code word to be delivered to me on the pitch if that happened. Luckily, it didn't, and on 24 July 2006 our son Lorenz was born in Wythenshawe Hospital in Manchester.

Nothing anyone says can prepare you for the intensity of love that floods every fibre of your being when you hold your first child in your arms. Pure, unconditional love poured out of me. I didn't cry – but in that moment, for perhaps the first time in my life, seeing Rebecca and Lorenz together, something other than football suddenly meant everything to me.

Rebecca with baby Lorenz

Rebecca, too, was transformed. If she had ever had any doubts about whether motherhood would suit her, they had vanished. For the first three months of Lorenz's life she barely even left the house, and God help anyone who came near the baby without sanitising their hands first. She wielded bottles of the stuff like pistols. 'Have you washed your hands?' she would interrogate visitors. 'Seriously, *have* you washed your hands?' Overnight she turned into Supermum, and once Lorenz was weaned I would come home from training to find the kitchen looking like a baby-food factory. She was adamant that nothing but home-made food would pass his lips, and must have puréed more sweet potato than a Cow & Gate production line.

Like most new mums, Rebecca was a big worrier. Lorenz

was far from an easy baby: he used to scream the house down, and in the early weeks and months he ran Rebecca ragged. Concerned about the endless crying, she sought professional advice, but putting it into practice wasn't easy for her. To stop him yelling all night, she was advised not to go to him every time he erupted, but it took all her will-power to resist taking him in her arms as soon as he made a sound.

She understood the importance of structure for babies, and became meticulously disciplined about maintaining a routine. She baby-proofed every inch of the house, and layered every hard surface with spongy, jigsaw-style floor tiles to protect him against bumps and scrapes. I think becoming a mother helped Rebecca understand my own mum better. Suddenly my mother's lioness-like protectiveness made sense to her, because Rebecca was exactly the same. She would not have dreamed of employing a nanny, and sometimes even worried about whether *I* was up to looking after Lorenz. She used to fret that I might take him out somewhere, get distracted and wander off without him. (Just for the record, yes, I am no-toriously forgetful, but Rebecca had nothing to worry about when it came to Lorenz. I could have no sooner forgotten him than left my own head behind.)

It would have been impossible for fatherhood not to change my perspective on life. After a poor performance I could no longer come home glowering and stare in silence at a TV screen for ten hours. I couldn't let my kids see me like that. I forced myself to leave football behind when I got home: I wanted them to see me positive and upbeat, not morose and monosyllabic.

With Lorenz

Rebecca had worried about my ability to show my children love. She knew the atmosphere I had grown up in, and would say to me, 'How are you going to be with your kids? When we have kids, say we have kids, are you going to be cold towards them?'

'What are you talking about?'

'You don't get it, do you?' she persisted. 'Once you have kids, you've got to say, "I love you," to them, and cuddle them.' I thought about my dad, and began to see her point.

'Are you going to be like that? Do you want your kids to feel about you the way you did about him when you were young?'

It hits home when you hear it put like that. No. I did not want to be like that, and I did not want them to feel like that either.

Funnily enough, Rebecca turned out to be the stricter parent of the two of us. Because I was absent so much for football, she often had to be both Mum and Dad, and was militant about manners and discipline. We had both seen famous parents raise thoughtless, disrespectful kids, and she was very clear that this was never going to be true of ours. She was an astonishing mum – tirelessly committed, endlessly loving, intuitively wise. I get how women often feel conflicted about motherhood: they love and resent it simultaneously, for although they adore their children, they also fear losing their own identity. But for Rebecca, there was no conflict. From the day Lorenz was born all she wanted from life was to take care of her children.

She certainly wasn't interested in being a WAG. Towards the other players' wives and girlfriends she was friendly enough, but never got involved in coffees and lunches. 'Why would I want to do that,' she used to say, 'when I've got my kids to look after?' People often describe the WAG scene as competitive and bitchy, but I have no idea if that is really true or not because Rebecca paid no attention: she didn't care what anyone thought of her. In that respect, we were very similar. Her family was her focus, and she could be quite cold towards anyone she didn't consider a friend. The fact that someone happened to be married to her husband's friend or teammate meant nothing to her. If Rebecca had some free time during the day she liked to drop in for a cup of tea with our housekeeper, Sandra.

My agent, Jamie, received a constant stream of requests from celebrity magazines for 'at home' photo shoots and lifestyle interviews. He knew better than to bother passing them on: Rebecca would no sooner have invited press photographers into our home than asked the BNP to tea. She loathed the paparazzi, and kept herself so far below the radar that few of them were even entirely sure what she looked like.

'Are you Mrs Ferdinand?' one yelled to her once, when she was out shopping.

Pointing towards a random street, she called back, 'No – but I've just seen her go that way!'

We received so many invitations to celebrity events that we could have gone out in black tie every night if we'd liked. Rebecca preferred to curl up on the sofa in her pyjamas with a girlfriend and a jumbo Galaxy bar and watch *Marley and Me*. She dreaded glitzy functions, and attended as few as we could get away with. Even the Man United end-of-season gala dinner felt like an unnecessary effort to her. She had no time for fans bothering us when we were out with the family, and would give autograph hunters abruptly short shrift.

We were almost uncannily compatible. I think I could count the major arguments we had on the fingers of one hand, and we never raised our voices in front of the kids. From my own experience as a child, I knew how frightening it could be to hear your parents rowing, and we made sure ours didn't have to endure it. If we argued, it tended to be over trivial things. My forgetfulness used to drive her nuts, and the one thing that used to annoy me about Rebecca was her habit of asking, 'Does my bum look big in this?' She was an unusually confident character, but if she had one insecurity it was her post-pregnancy weight.

'How does this look on me?' she would ask, peering doubtfully at her reflection.

'Do you honestly want me to tell you? Or do you want me to say what you want to hear?'

'Tell me honestly.'

'Okay then. It's not you. It doesn't suit your figure.'

And without fail, like clockwork every time, all hell would break loose.

It would be absurd to pretend we didn't have our ups and downs. Like every couple, we had our moments when one or both of us would think, *Fucking hell, what* is going on here? One of the hardest things for Rebecca were press reports and social media rumours of my infidelity. They cut her to the quick. I wasn't a saint, and I made some mistakes, and I really regret the press they got which put Rebecca through so much additional pain.

Until the day she died, there was only ever one important girl in my life, and I think Rebecca always knew that. But the heartbreaking fact is that I was never able to overcome the cold emotional distance that had become second nature to me long before we ever met. Behind closed doors I could cope with snuggling up in front of the telly, but even holding hands in front of anyone made me excruciatingly uncomfortable. Apart from our kids, nobody – not even our parents – would have seen Rebecca and me kiss or cuddle.

Because I saw no love between my mum and dad, I found the simplest expression of affection beyond me. Rebecca told me she loved me all the time, and couldn't understand why I found it so hard. 'I love you,' she would say, 'so of course I'm going to tell you. Why can't you do that for me?'

'But I can't.' I'd squirm, almost laughing with embarrassment.

'Well, then, you don't love me.'

'But you know I do.'

'Then why can't you say it?'

'Don't you know I love you? Why do I have to say it every day?' To be completely honest, I found her longing to hear the words a little bit needy. Why would I do that? I would wonder. Why should I even be thinking about it? I can't win a trophy by doing that. It's a waste of time. In my head I was always so wrapped up in football, I simply couldn't see the point of repeating something Rebecca had already heard.

Out loud I would ask, 'Why are we even having this conversation again?'

'Okay,' Rebecca would say. 'I do know you love me. But I need you to show it. I need to feel it.'

'But I've told you already. Why are we even chatting? I don't understand.' If my mind had not always been on football, maybe I would have stopped to *hear* what she was saying. To me now, it seems extraordinary that I wouldn't just give her what she needed. But I didn't, because I couldn't.

Rebecca would always want to talk a disagreement through, whereas I was stubborn and would rather brood. If I'm put under pressure, I simply close down – and, again, it's a measure of her strength that she was able to override her impulse to keep pressing a point, and instead give me space. In the early days my coldness was bewildering to her. 'Why are you like this?' she'd ask. 'Why are you so hard to get close to?' Over the years, as she understood more about my background, everything made more sense to her. But in the beginning I didn't even understand what she was talking about. I thought I was normal.

Even explaining to her why I was the way I was went against all my instincts. Ever since I can remember, I have been intensely secretive. 'You tell me just enough,' Rebecca would say. 'You never tell me more than you absolutely need to.' It wasn't conscious or deliberate on my part: I just didn't know any other way.

Rebecca knew me better than anyone. 'Rio,' she would say, 'I know you care about certain things – but I know only because I know you. You don't show it. I don't know if inside you're going bananas about something because you just don't show it. I never know what you're thinking.'

People have been saying that to me all my life. 'We don't know what you're thinking. We don't know what you're feeling.' And the saddest thing is, I used to take it as a compliment. I used to be proud of it.

CHAPTER EIGHT

Best-laid Plans

IT IS 27 June 2009. I am standing on a beach on a tiny private island in the British Virgin Isles. Our families are here, and our closest friends. Everywhere I turn I see faces I love. I can see Lorenz in his little white suit, matching mine. Our second son, Tate, is not yet one, and is all dressed up, sitting in his carry-cot. A Caribbean breeze cools us as we wait; the palm trees twist and bend as if they're dancing. Eva Cassidy's 'Songbird' drifts across the warm air, and all eyes turn to the bride.

Rebecca doesn't so much step towards me on her father's arm as float. She takes my breath away. Her beauty is unreal – iridescent – and she glimmers and shines and glows as she takes her place by my side. A tear streams down my cheek. I want this moment to last for ever. I have never been more in love, or felt luckier.

I DIDN'T THINK I would get married. My parents hadn't, and neither had pretty much anyone else in my family. Weddings

125

weren't part of my life or my background, and it was really only for this reason that I couldn't see myself standing in front of people saying, 'I do.'

Rebecca wanted a wedding, but I don't think she imagined it would ever happen either. After Lorenz was born she brought it up. 'What – so you can have a kid with me, but you won't marry me?' I stuck to my guns. In my mind it was children who signified real commitment, not a ring. Weddings were not me, and that was that.

But by 2007, I found myself slowly coming around to the idea. We were a family now, and I liked the thought of connecting us together formally. It felt right. Naturally, I didn't tell Rebecca about my change of heart, but I did call her dad to tell him I was going to propose. Once I'd decided to do this thing, I wanted to do it properly.

Well, I say 'properly'. Exactly how it happened might not be everybody's idea of 'proper'. That summer I went away to Las Vegas with some of my teammates, and we went out on one almighty bender. A day of drinking turned into a night, and the following morning I was still in a casino when we were invited to a pool party. I can't remember very much about the party, except that by then my phone battery had died, and I asked a total stranger if I could borrow his mobile to call Rebecca. It was in the days before iPhones, when if your battery died you would pop your Sim card into someone else's handset – which was what I did. I have no memory of the phone call, and must have crawled into bed some time around lunchtime.

It was the following afternoon when I woke up. I checked my phone. There was a message from Rebecca. *Right. I've booked the flight. We're on our way.*

What? Why was she coming? Her message said she was bringing Lorenz, and a friend, and ended, with: 'This had better be a good surprise.'

I lay back in bed, scratching my sore head, staring at the phone. What did she mean? Slowly, the penny began to drop. In my drunken state I had called Rebecca and told her to get to Vegas ASAP because I had a big surprise waiting for her. I checked the time. Oh, my God. Rebecca would be arriving the following day: I had less than twenty-four hours to find a ring.

Luckily I was friends with an American-football player who knew a jeweller in Vegas. I got on the phone to him at once, and he came to my hotel with the most beautiful ring. Perfect. But where were we even going to stay? Rebecca was about to arrive with a girlfriend and our son. They could hardly all sleep in my hotel room. Again, luck was on my side. I knew the general manager of the hotel, told him I needed one of their villas, and within an hour my bags were packed and being moved by the concierge.

Rebecca arrived, a bit bleary with jetlag but bursting with curiosity. 'So what is it, then?' she kept asking, laughing. I sent her friend out, and ordered in a private chef to barbecue dinner for us. Once Lorenz was settled into his high chair, I placed the ring box in front of him. He picked it up and began playing with it.

'What's that?' Rebecca asked, confused for a moment as she spotted him lift the box to his mouth and give it an experimental bite. 'What's he playing with?'

Then she saw. As she registered what Lorenz was holding, I slipped out of my chair beside her, went down on one knee, retrieved the ring from Lorenz and took Rebecca's hand.

'Rebecca. Will you marry me?'

I'd love to pretend the proposal took her by surprise, and she played along, looking astonished and bowled over, but, honestly, I suspect she knew exactly why she was coming to Vegas. When I had made the drunken call from the pool party, I can't imagine I was particularly mysterious or discreet. But I didn't care. All that mattered to me was that she said yes.

Rebecca's mum had been bursting with excitement ever since I'd told her dad I was going to propose. Now that I'd finally done it, she couldn't wait to start planning the wedding with her daughter, and as organisation is my idea of a nightmare you won't be surprised to hear that I was very happy to leave them to it.

The only request I made was that the wedding take place abroad. I come from an enormous family, and know a lot of people, so it was easy to see how the guest list could get out of hand or turn into a diplomatic minefield. Getting married abroad would solve a lot of problems, so that was what we agreed. Beyond that – oh, and the music, which mattered a lot to me – as with the rest of our domestic life, the wedding was Rebecca's department.

Rebecca with her mum

Planning it was a phenomenal operation, and took nearly two years. In 2008 Tate was born, and our hearts were stolen all over again. Lorenz took after Rebecca's side of the family in his appearance, but Tate looked exactly like me, and with two children we now felt even more like a family. How

Rebecca managed to organise a wedding while taking care of a baby and a toddler is a mystery. On top of all that, she was determined to lose the baby weight from Tate, and practically starved herself to get down to a size ten wedding dress. Privately I thought the dieting was mad, and totally unnecessary, but knew better than to interfere.

Privacy was one of the biggest challenges, and in order to keep the press away we didn't tell a soul where the wedding was going to happen. Guests received invitations in passport holders, with instructions on what they should pack: sunglasses, swimwear, evening wear. We planned a blessing for Tate to take place the day after the wedding, so told everyone they would need two outfits, but other than that we kept them in the dark right up until they got on the plane.

We invited a hundred guests, and chartered a private aeroplane. Everyone was told to come to Gatwick airport, and even when they boarded the flight they still didn't know the destination. Once the plane was in the air, we screened a video Rebecca and I had filmed in our kitchen, announcing where they were going and what would be happening.

Obviously I'm biased, but it was the best wedding I've ever been to. To have a hundred of your closest family and friends together on a private Caribbean island for five days, with decks set up in the bar and on the beach and your mates DJing all day and night – it doesn't get much better than that. I'm not one for making speeches, but I've been writing poetry ever since I got into rap music in my twenties. For our wedding I wrote Rebecca a love poem, and read it out instead of a speech.

Two years later, Tia was born. Rebecca was so excited to have a girl that she sent her mum straight off to John Lewis to buy up every single pink thing in the shop. I was completely unprepared for the impact a daughter would have on my heart. Rebecca used to call her our dumpling, because Tia was something of a bruiser as a baby, but the tenderness I found hidden in my heart for a little girl came as the sweetest shock to me.

By 2013 the end of my career was drawing near. Jamie had found a plot of land for us to build on near Orpington, less than a mile from the house where he lived with his wife Lisa and their kids. By then Rebecca and Lisa had become best friends. Our children were the same age, and because I could never come away on holiday, Rebecca and the kids often went away with them. We were a tight foursome, and the thought that in a few years we would all be living practically next door to each other filled the future with excitement and hope.

After all these years in the north, we would soon be coming home. Rebecca and I designed and built our house in Orpington from scratch; it was another massive project that she took care of, and Rebecca loved every minute. She was in her element. It was, as she liked to say, going to be our forever home.

IT DIDN'T SOUND like a major drama when she told me she'd found a lump. 'It's probably nothing,' she said briskly, almost breezily. 'I'll get the doctor to have a look, but I don't think it's anything to worry about.'

At least, I think that's what she said. As you are going to see shortly, what I was able to take in and what actually happened do not always turn out to be the same thing.

What I do know is that we were relaxed enough about the situation for Rebecca to go and see the GP by herself. It was the autumn of 2013, and I was still playing for Man United. The appointment must have been at around lunchtime, because I was driving home from training when she called. I remember approaching Alderley Edge roundabout, near our house, when my mobile rang. It was Rebecca. She was sobbing hysterically, but managed to get a few words out.

'Rio. It's cancer. I've got breast cancer.'

The rest of the drive home is a blur. All I can remember is having to resist the impulse to ram the car off the road. In fact, I don't remember very much about the first few days after her diagnosis. I know we drove down to her parents' house in Essex with her sister, and can remember the expression of surprise, quickly followed by concern, on her mother's face when she opened the door to find us outside. Telling her mum she had cancer must have been one of the hardest things Rebecca ever had to do. She took her upstairs to a bedroom, while we sat in shell-shocked silence in the living room and listened to their cries.

'I'm not going to see Tia grow up,' Rebecca kept saying. 'I just have this feeling inside me now that I'm not going to see my kids grow up. Tia won't even remember me.' She had a type of breast cancer known as Triple Negative, the most aggressive form of the disease. As she told her mum, 'It's the worst type. It's got hands, and it's travelling.' To her sister she kept saying, 'I'm not going to survive this. My body's not going to make old bones.' She was one of the strongest women I've ever met, but in those early days not even Rebecca could find the strength to believe in her future.

She was booked in for a double mastectomy in two weeks' time, and would then need months of chemotherapy. She spent the fortnight getting the house ready for her absence, and within days her old spirit began to return. She ordered wigs, and had her eyebrows tattooed in preparation for when they would fall out. 'I'm going to fight this. I'm going to get through it,' she promised.

But she was frantically worried about losing her hair, and frightened of being disfigured. 'You didn't sign up to this, Rio,' she kept telling me. 'You're not going to like me any more after all of this. You're not going to want to be with someone like this. You're going to want to be with someone else.'

I didn't know it at the time, but this was the big fear she was confiding to the tight circle of people we told about her cancer. 'My skin will be old and wrinkly and Rio won't want to look at me,' she told them. 'I'll give him a way out. I'll make it okay for him to go. He won't want this.'

If I could turn back the clock I'd give anything to be able to reassure and soothe her – but at the time her fear sounded so ridiculous to me, all I could say was: 'Shut up. Don't be stupid.' I loved her and nothing was going to change that so I couldn't understand how she could even think it. Privately, I would not allow myself to think about what the doctors were about to do to her body. Like all negative thoughts, I simply shut it out.

Her mum took her to hospital for the operation. When I saw her after the surgery, the shock was devastating: she had a morphine drip, and the drug had been making her hallucinate. Surgical drains were still attached to her – strange contraptions that looked bizarrely like a home-made wine-making kit, with plastic tubing running from her wounds into clear jars where pale fluid dripped and slowly gathered. It was horrifying, and heartbreaking.

She was mortified when the chemo began and her hair fell out. As soon as the first clumps came away in her hand, she took herself off to the bedroom and shaved her head herself. She had warned the children this would happen, and made a big joke of her wigs, laughing, 'Look, it's growing back!' Throughout all those grim months of treatment, her only priority was to spare the children, so much so that they were under the impression cancer was nothing worse than a cold.

Not once did she allow herself to become emotional in front of them. After each round of chemo she would be unable to get out of bed, but as soon as she could she would be up and pottering around the house, making cheese on toast, summoning a heroic effort to make everything appear normal for the children. All she ever thought about was their needs.

'I cannot let them see me going under,' she would say to me, after they were in bed. 'They are not going to see me fail.' I'd always thought I was someone who knew how to front out fear, but Rebecca put on the bravest face I have ever seen, and my respect for her went beyond anything words could say. She had such bullet-proof courage, I never once feared that she would not get through it.

We had just bought our holiday home in Portugal when she was diagnosed. At first she considered pulling out of the sale, but instead threw herself into the project to get her through chemo, and when she was well enough between rounds she would fly out with her mum or her sister to make it the home she had always dreamed of. She kept her mind fixed firmly on the future. I'd be retiring soon, and finally we would be able to go away as a family for the summer holidays. She wanted us to have the perfect home, and filled every inch of that house with her personality and style.

She was desperate to keep her illness a secret – and, being Rebecca, she managed it. The children were sworn to secrecy, and even the woman who came most days to do the ironing had no idea, until one day she happened to find one of Rebecca's wigs drying on a stand. At home, Rebecca would wear a turban, but she never left the house without a wig, and always looked stunning. No one could have guessed there were days when the chemo had played such havoc with her mouth that she couldn't even taste a Malteser, or that her gums and nails hurt so much she wanted to scream.

And me? By now you can probably guess how I coped. I went to work, kept training, kept playing and kept my mind on football. The only teammate I told was Nemanja Vidić. Sir Alex Ferguson was retiring from the club, David Moyes was taking over as the new manager, and as they were my bosses I felt I had to tell them. But to no one else in the football world did I breathe a word.

Looking back now, I sometimes wonder whether the secrecy played a part in helping me retreat into blank denial. For as long as nobody knew about it, a part of me could pretend to myself that it wasn't really happening. If Rebecca was frightened she didn't let me see it, and it's another testament to her selflessness and courage that I never came away from a conversation with her about the cancer worrying that it might break her.

Jamie thinks my sportsman's mindset must have played a big part in this, too, and I'm sure he's right. I was used to winning, not losing. I trusted in the universe I had always known, the one in which everything always turned out well.

And for a magical ten months, it looked as if this would too. Rebecca completed her treatment in the spring of 2014 and was declared well, and at the end of that season I left Man United.

Had it not been for her illness, this would have been one of the most momentous occasions of my life. I had been with the club for twelve years. It was my identity. It was in my DNA. The idea of ending my career at another Premier League club felt almost unimaginable.

Before Rebecca became ill, I had toyed with the idea of playing abroad for a year or two after leaving Man United. Clubs in the US and the Middle East had been lining up to sign me, and the prospect of a foreign finale was quite appealing. It would have been an adventure. But now there was only one option on the table. We had to go home. After what she had been through, Rebecca needed to be near her family. By a stroke of luck, my old manager and friend from West Ham, Harry Redknapp, was now managing another London club. I could sign with him for Queens Park Rangers and no one would ask any questions. On paper a lower-table club like QPR might have seemed a surprising choice for me, and could have raised some eyebrows, but everybody knew how far back Harry and I went, so no one would query it.

We moved south to our forever house that summer. Rebecca was overjoyed to be home. We had built a gym in the garden and she threw herself into training, determined to get herself back to health and fitness. Her birthday was on 5 December, and Jamie's fell three days beforehand, so in early December they threw a joint birthday party at a pub near our house. I'd have been surprised if more than a dozen of the guests had any idea she had been ill, and nobody there that night would have guessed. She looked electrifyingly beautiful – radiant and sparkling. Her hair had grown back enough for her to put away the wigs, and she carried off her crop with such style that everyone was bowled over by her stunning new look. It looked like the bold choice of a woman who knew she had the face to pull it off. No one had a clue that chemo had anything to do with it.

We tumbled home in the early hours in high spirits. It had been a blinding night. I remember putting crumpets in the toaster and going to hang up my coat in the hall. By the time I got back to the kitchen, Rebecca had eaten them. I chased her round the kitchen island, laughing, and she squealed with giggles and teased me by brushing away crumbs from her mouth.

We were a normal couple again, play-fighting over something as silly as crumpets. The nightmare of the previous year was over. We had everything to play for. Everything was going to be all right.

CHAPTER NINE

The Impossible Goodbye

IT IS EARLY March 2015. I'm driving across London with my QPR teammate Bobby Zamora in the car. It's a normal midweek morning, and we're on our way to work. In a few minutes we'll be at the training ground. The first hint of spring sunshine is creeping through the clouds over the city, and the stereo is playing some deep R&B. I have nothing in particular on my mind, but I'm in a good mood.

The phone rings. It's Rebecca's sister.

'Rio.' She's shrieking down the phone, breathless and frantic. 'Rebecca's collapsed. She's been taken into intensive care. Get here now.'

I screech to a halt and pull over. Bobby gets out. I turn the car and drive like a madman to the hospital in South Kensington, my mind flying through a thousand different scenarios. What the hell has happened? What is wrong with Rebecca? *What is going on?* I have no idea.

* * *

DO YOU REMEMBER that this is what I told you at the beginning of the book? Well, it's the story I've been telling myself for more than two years. Now here's the really strange thing. It's not true.

It's only through the process of writing this book that I've come to understand that what my mind has allowed me to remember has less to do with reality than with the power of denial. I cannot remember, it turns out, what I clearly could not bear.

I have learned the truth by piecing together the memories of everyone around me. This is what actually happened.

In January 2015 Rebecca began to complain of a bad back. She had been training hard in the gym, and I thought she was probably overdoing it. She was grumpy about it, and I was a little bit impatient. 'Just go to the GP and get it sorted,' I told her, thinking it sounded like a slipped disc. The other likely explanation was that she had recently had an injection at the Royal Marsden, where she went for her regular check-ups, to switch off her ovaries. It's a fairly standard procedure to prevent breast cancer coming back, but meant her body would be adjusting to the sudden disappearance of oestrogen, which might explain the aches and pains.

In early February she went to Portugal with her sister, who came back bewildered by Rebecca's irritability. Her mum was getting a little fed up with it too. 'You and your bloody back,' she would say. 'Take some more co-codamol and you'll be fine.'

Rebecca had been home from Portugal for a few days when she went upstairs to take a quick bath after dropping the boys at school. I was busy in the kitchen when I heard her calling me. There was an edge in her voice I had never heard before.

'Rio! Come up here, please. I need you.'

I found her lying rigid in the bath, her face twisted with pain.

'I can't get out. I've tried and I can't. I can't move.'

I tried gathering her in my arms to pull her out but all I seemed to do was make it worse. She was in agony, and I was scared to move her. At that moment the doorbell rang. It was Rebecca's mum, dropping round with Rebecca's aunt for a cup of tea. I let them in, then took her mum aside.

'Can I have a word with you? She's upstairs in the bath – but she can't get out. She's in so much pain I can't move her. I don't know what to do.'

Her mum went upstairs and found Rebecca as I had left her. She took one look, and the problem seemed to be reasonably straightforward: the muscles that had been playing up in her back must have gone into spasm. Somehow she helped Rebecca out of the bath, and onto her bed.

'Oh, Mum, it's agony,' gasped Rebecca. 'It's like my bones hurt and I don't know what to do.'

'Right,' her mum said. 'Take some more of your co-codamol, and we'll see how it goes. But we've got to get you to the doctor. This is obviously getting bad.'

'Well,' Rebecca said, 'I've got a check-up appointment booked for next week anyway, so we can ask them then.' Within half an hour she was back on her feet and appeared absolutely fine. She had lunch and went out shopping with her mum and aunt. The drama was over.

Her mum went with her to hospital the following week.

The doctor examined her back and did not seem unduly alarmed. 'Well, I can't feel anything amiss. But we'll take some bloods, and I'll arrange a scan.'

But the Royal Marsden radiography department was fully booked. Non-emergency cases like Rebecca's, the hospital staff explained, would have to wait a little while. Her mum worked as a nurse in a private hospital in Essex so quickly got on the phone to work. 'If we jump in the car and head up there, is there any chance someone could give my daughter a scan then and there?'

'Sure, no problem. We'll see you soon.'

On the way to the hospital in Essex, Rebecca received a call from the Royal Marsden. They had her blood test results and were slightly concerned because her tumour markers were up. These indicate the possibility of cancer cells in the body – but could also signify nothing more sinister than the after-effects of the breast-reconstruction surgery Rebecca had undergone a few months earlier.

'Probably nothing to worry about,' the doctor reassured her. 'But we'll be quite keen to see the results of that scan once they come through.'

After the scan Rebecca could barely get up off the bed. The pain was back, and with a vengeance. She must have told me all of this when she got home that evening, but I have literally no memory of it.

The following morning her mum collected the scan report and delivered it to the Royal Marsden. I was off work that day, and Rebecca and I made the journey to the Royal Marsden together to learn the results of the scan. I can tell you nothing about the shock of receiving the news: I've simply blanked it. But the scan had found tumours and lesions in her spine. The diagnosis was unequivocal. The cancer had come back.

Her mum was waiting by the phone when Rebecca called. 'It's really bad, Mum. Really, really bad.' My mum says I howled down the line like a wild animal when I broke the news to her, struggling to get the words out through my tears. Jamie says I was practically deranged with panic when I spoke to him. We drove home while Rebecca's mum and dad tore across town. They arrived shortly after us.

'I'm going to die, Mum,' she told her mother, sitting on our bed, sobbing. 'I'm going to die this time. There's not much they can do. They said they might be able to give me a little bit of time, but I am going to die.'

'No, you are *not,*' her mum told her. 'You're going to be fine. They can give you enough time for them to find something that's going to make you better.'

The following morning I took Rebecca back to the Royal Marsden to have a blood transfusion and radiotherapy. Rebecca's mum says I was barely even present, staring blindly into space, like a rabbit in the headlights. Rebecca sent her mum out to buy new wigs, and I stayed with her while radiotherapy was administered, before taking her home.

At dawn the following morning I phoned her mum. 'I don't know what to do. She's screaming with pain. She's in so much pain I don't know what to do.' I called the Royal Marsden. Rebecca's mum raced to Orpington, and by the time she arrived the hospital had called back to say they had a bed ready. We managed to get Rebecca onto the back seat of the car and drove her to hospital. When we arrived she was writhing in agony and the nurses struggled to get lines into her veins, battling to get pain relief into her system as fast as possible.

Later that afternoon I left Rebecca with her mum and went home to look after the kids. Rebecca had a terrible night, half out of her mind with pain, but by the morning the doctors had managed to get it under control, and when her sister arrived, her mum returned to our house to collect some clothes.

She was at the house when the chilling call came from hospital.

'Mum.' It was Rebecca's sister. 'They've taken her into intensive care. Get back up here as quick as you can. They think she's going to die.' And that was when Rebecca's sister called me.

It is as if my memory has simply auto-deleted more than a week of my life, like wiping clean an old cassette. From the day Rebecca couldn't get out of the bath, to the day her sister called me, the tape is pretty much blank.

But I see now that my mind went to even greater lengths than that to protect me from the horror of what was taking place. Because just hours before Rebecca was rushed into intensive care and nearly died, I had got up and *gone to work.*

BY THE TIME Rebecca came out of intensive care, the full gravity of the situation was known. The cancer had spread not just to her bones but her bone marrow and her liver. The prognosis was unambiguous: she was dying.

And yet, in my mind, that was not what was happening. Each week there would be new treatments and talk of experimental drugs, and I seized upon each one like a lifeline. I simply could not process the stark fact that her condition was terminal. Maybe they'll be able to keep the cancer in a box, I kept saying. They'll be able to contain it, and give her at least ten years' good-quality life. It was pure fantasy – of course it was – but a necessary fantasy to sustain me through the darkest eight weeks I have ever known. For as long as there was life, there had to be hope.

This mindset also helped me keep up a surreal performance of normality at home in front of the children. Rebecca was determined to protect them from the agony of her ordeal, so I told them she was a bit poorly but would be better soon, and did everything I could not to disrupt their daily routine. Sandra, our old housekeeper from Manchester, moved into our house, and so did my mum, while Rebecca's mum set up a camp bed in her hospital room. She had to get up early each morning to wash and brush her teeth in the public toilets before the ward filled with visitors, but not once did she complain. It must have been unimaginably awful to have to watch her daughter dying, but she never left Rebecca's side, and this allowed me to maintain some sort of semblance of ordinary life at home for the children.

It sounds almost implausible now, but the kids really did appear to be fairly untroubled. Tia was still at nursery, so twice a week my mum would drive her up to hospital to have lunch with Rebecca, then dash back in time to collect the boys from school. The boys would come up two or three times a week after school, and Rebecca always tried to time her drugs so that she could be alert for the children's visits. She would play doctors with them, and let them play with the nurses' gloves, and sometimes there were even days when she was well enough to leave her bed and take a walk to a café near South Kensington station. Lorenz became suspicious about my red eyes whenever he came to the hospital, but I told him it must be hay fever from a plant in Mummy's room.

'Better get that plant out of Mum's room, Dad,' he suggested one afternoon, studying my face closely, 'cos it's making your hay fever really bad.' Maybe he knew a lot more than he was letting on. Apart from that moment, though, the kids appeared to be satisfied with the version of events they were getting: Mum was not well, but she would get better, and soon she'd be coming home.

Sometimes Rebecca would be too drugged to open her eyes when I came, and I would sit for hours with her, watching her sleep. I come from a Christian family, but watching Rebecca lie there in that hospital bed I found myself questioning God. All these people believe in Him – and He allows this to happen? How is that possible? I found it very hard to believe in a God who was supposed to be all powerful, knew this was happening but chose to do nothing to help.

The people truly helping were the nursing staff. They were heroic. Rebecca used to joke around with them, taking the mickey out of them and herself, and as the weeks passed they grew closer and closer. I didn't know it at the time, but very few patients stay on that ward for long. They are usually dead within a fortnight.

Mind you, Rebecca did take a violent dislike to one hospital staff member. I was with her one afternoon when a knock came on the door. A young woman poked her head in. 'Can I come in?' She smiled, all bright and breezy. She was a counsellor, she explained, and had come to talk to us about therapeutic support available to families in our situation. Rebecca took against her on sight.

'Tell me this,' she asked her coldly. 'Have you ever lost someone close to you?'

'Well, no, I can't say I have,' the young woman replied. 'But I have trained.'

Without another word, Rebecca shifted onto her side to face the wall, and after a few awkward minutes the counsellor backed sheepishly out of the room.

'Don't let her anywhere near my kids,' Rebecca told me flatly, once she had gone. 'What the hell does she know? She's never had to live through anything like this. What a pointless waste of time.'

As her condition worsened, the doctors remained upbeat, if increasingly vague, when talking to Rebecca. 'We've got this new treatment to try next,' they would say encouragingly, after yet another had failed.

'Am I fucked?' she asked bluntly.

'No, no, don't worry, we'll give you every best chance here.'

But privately, with myself and her family, the medical staff grew gloomier. 'Listen,' the consultant would say, looking serious. 'Things are very difficult now.' And yet, looking back, I realise Rebecca was probably the only one of all of us who could face the fact that she was dying.

She tried to talk to her mother and sister about it, and tried to tell them about her heartbreak that she wouldn't live to enjoy the homes and life she had created for her family, but it was more than they could bear. 'You're not going anywhere,' they would promise her. 'You are not going to die.' Her father somehow found it in him to let her talk about dying sometimes, and with him Rebecca spent hours going through practicalities – computer passwords, Portugal house details, domestic minutiae. These conversations must have been a kind of torture for him, and I've no idea how he managed to get through them.

I didn't know this at the time, but she even talked to him about flying to Switzerland to end her life at Dignitas. 'I don't want to string this out, Dad,' she told him. 'If I can't get out of bed to see my kids, I don't want to be here.'

He reasoned patiently with her – 'You can't do that, you can't give up' – and of course events overtook us before she could mention Dignitas again.

Rebecca and her father shared a similar dark sense of humour, and in the final days I think this became her coping mechanism. One afternoon he was with her when a nurse popped her head around the door to say a visitor had just arrived.

'Quick, Dad,' Rebecca joked. 'Pull the sheet over my head before they come in and pretend I've just died!'

To her sister she would say, 'Come on, you know I'm going to die. And you know what you're like with clothes. So you'd better start sorting out your outfit now, because you won't know what to wear.'

My coping mechanism was drink. I was still playing for QPR, but other than Bobby Zamora, who had been in the car with me when that fateful phone call came, only the manager knew about Rebecca's illness. He had told me not to come to work unless I wanted to, but as part of the performance of normality for the children I tried to keep training. If I wasn't at home looking after them, or in hospital with Rebecca, I was at the club trying to carry on doing my job. But my heart was not in it, and my form nosedived, to the point where fans and reporters began questioning my place in the squad. For the first time in my life, I didn't care.

I hadn't been a big drinker for well over a decade, not since I had joined Man United. Now I was drinking a beer or two every night, even before a game. One week in March, I was told the team had a couple of injuries and there was an outside chance they might need me to play. I joined the team in a hotel on the South Bank the night before the match, but it felt bizarre to be going through the motions of impersonating someone who cared about football, so after dinner I put on a baseball cap and headphones and headed out for a stroll towards Westminster. I walked for more than four hours, and to this day I have no idea where I went or what I did. Jamie was trying to get hold of me and became increasingly frantic as my phone remained offline – which anyone who knows me will tell you is unheard of. I got back to the hotel at half past midnight and had something to drink – and was selected to play the next day. This was not the right preparation the night before a game. I sleep-walked through it, and we lost 3–0.

At some deep level I must have known the truth of what was about to happen. I didn't let myself get emotional or lose control in front of Rebecca or the kids, but with Jamie or my parents I occasionally cracked and cried tears of panic, and my subconscious must have been in turmoil: I developed severe insomnia and had to take pills to get to sleep. My conscious daytime self, however, couldn't face the truth, least of all with Rebecca. She came home from hospital only twice in the final weeks of her life, and during her first visit she tried to talk to me. I remember it as though it was yesterday.

I was lying on our bed, staring vacantly at the television. She was in the bathroom.

'You know what kills me?' she called to me. 'Over all these years I've helped to mould you into someone who's going to be a great husband for someone else now.' Her words burned me like acid.

'What you talking about?' I called back sharply. I was afraid if I turned my gaze away from the screen I would start to cry. 'What you talking about? Shut up.'

She appeared in the bathroom door, tears rolling down her cheeks, and came and lay beside me on the bed. 'Listen, there's a big chance I'm not going to get through this. We need to start thinking about it. We need to talk about it.'

'What you chatting about?'

She began to get angry, raising her voice, but I kept staring at the TV, zoning out. 'You don't get it, do you? You don't realise, do you? I don't think you realise how serious this is.'

Did I, or didn't I? I don't even know. All I know is that this conversation was beyond me. For my entire life as a sportsman, I had trained my mind to think only of winning. It is what I had been conditioned to do. Negative thoughts were strictly forbidden: if you allow yourself to start thinking about losing, you probably will. In life you have to prepare for all eventualities – but not in football. I could not differentiate between real life and a football pitch, and only knew how to prepare myself to win.

I stared at the screen and closed the conversation down. She never tried again.

Rebecca came home one final time before she died, for Tia's fourth birthday party. Rebecca had always thrown elaborately magical birthday parties for the children, and didn't want Tia to miss out this time. It was a miracle she even managed the car journey. By then her liver was failing and her limbs were swelling; her body was covered with bruises and she was suffering explosive nosebleeds. And yet, once again, almost all of the party guests were in the dark. Those who knew she had been a bit unwell were under the vague impression she was being treated for a slipped disc.

She kept having to retreat to the bedroom to plug another nosebleed and rest on the bed. Unbelievably, when the time came for the birthday cake, Rebecca lifted Tia so she could blow out her candles. I watched her kiss her daughter, and circulate around the garden making sure everyone was having a good time, and felt as if I couldn't breathe. She was in unfathomable pain by that point, and must have known she was close to death, yet still she could do this for her family.

I think she had held onto life so she could see Tia turn four. It was the last time the children saw her fully conscious and alert, and in the days that followed she deteriorated rapidly. Before a week was out, the doctors told us to gather her loved ones at the hospital, and break the news to her children that their mum was dying.

On Friday, 1 May, I sat in the room adjacent to Rebecca's

with my father, my brother Anton, Jamie and a bottle of brandy. Rebecca lay unconscious, her parents, brother and sister at her bedside. All day I drifted between the two rooms, half mad with grief and disbelief, waiting for the inevitable.

At ten thirty that evening Rebecca's brother appeared at the door.

'You'd better come now.'

As if we were walking towards our own execution, Anton, Dad and I joined Rebecca's family at her deathbed. I stood at the head of the bed, leaning over my wife's fragile body, wrapped my arms around her and held her as she died.

Rebecca always made sure to have a notebook to hand at the children's birthdays, to record who had given what so that they could write thank-you cards to everyone. She was scrupulous about thank-you cards, and this birthday was no exception. During Tia's party, as presents were unwrapped, she had carefully entered the names and details of the gifts in the book. It wasn't until weeks later that her mum opened it, ready to write the thank-you cards as Rebecca would have wanted.

But there were no names or gifts written on the page. It was just pure gibberish. The drugs had addled her brain to the point where she could no longer form words on the page. And yet still, for her daughter, Rebecca had tried.

CHAPTER TEN

Lost in Grief

I am at home, upstairs in the bedroom. It is late May 2015, and the kids are all at school. Sandra is out shopping. The house is quiet. I have been dreading doing this, but can't put it off for ever. I need to sort out Rebecca's things from the Royal Marsden.

I don't know who packed up her belongings and brought them home from the hospital. It certainly wasn't me. I was in no state to take care of anything. But somebody had done it, and her bags have been sitting on the floor of the bedroom ever since. I don't want to do this when the children are back later. I know I won't do it after they've gone to bed: I'll want a drink instead. I can tell myself I'll do it tomorrow morning, after dropping them at school   but I know I won't. I've been telling myself that every day for weeks now, and every day it doesn't happen. Pull yourself together, Rio. Let's just do this now. I take a deep breath.

The handbag is the last one I ever bought for Rebecca. Inside are two greetings cards. From the humour of the cartoons on the front, I can guess who she chose them for.

They were meant for me. Throughout our marriage, we had sometimes found it easier to say important things to each other in cards than with spoken words. She must have bought these in the final weeks of her life, and intended to write something to me inside them. But they are still in their cellophane wrapping. Whatever it was she had wanted to say, she didn't get the chance.

It gets worse when I open her suitcase. Tucked among her clothes I find half a dozen A5 hardback notebooks, the kind you might buy from WHSmith. Inside are crisp, white, lined pages. I can guess what they were for, and why she bought them. These were notepads she wanted to fill with instructions and advice to help me after she was gone. One by one, I open them. The pages are all blank. She did not have time.

I kneel on the floor and I sob.

GUILT IS A frighteningly powerful emotion. In my case, it was all the more intense because until Rebecca died I don't think I had ever really experienced it. It isn't something a sportsman would allow himself to feel: it's too dangerous, too potentially debilitating. And now I was drowning in it.

You might think I would have felt guilty for all the years I was away at football, leaving Rebecca to take care of everything alone. You might think I would have felt guilty about inviting friends up to Manchester for a big Saturday night out – then staring at the TV in silence for hours because I had played badly. You might think I felt guilty for missing Tia's birth.

But I didn't. In my mind, these things were a shame, of

course, but they were just the price we had to pay for me being the best at my job. The better a player I was, the better my family's life would be. That was how I always thought about it. One day I was going to retire, and then I would have the next thirty, forty, who knows, maybe even fifty years to repay Rebecca for all the sacrifices she had made. But that wasn't going to happen now. So, for the first time in my life, I found myself undone by guilt.

Each night, after the children were in bed, I sat in the living room in this great big empty house, looking around me and thinking, Why have I got this now? What is the point of this? This house was meant for the five of us. There should be noise and laughter. Rebecca should be asking me to do all the things I never could.

'Rio, would you paint this for me? Rio, could you clear out the garage? Rio, could you clean the barbecue?' I'm not training now. I'm not away with the team. I'm not upstairs resting. I'm here to do all those things for her – and she isn't here to ask me. The person who created all this, and deserved to enjoy it, isn't here. So what is the fucking point of it?

The guilt had started in the hospital, during the final weeks of her life. 'Do you think,' she had asked, 'I liked going away with the kids by myself all those years? Do you think I wanted to do that? I didn't want to do that. For all those years, I was looking forward to when you'd retired, and we'd go away for the summer as a family. We'd spend half-terms together, like normal families. Do you know how much I wanted that?' That was when the guilt set in.

I had to live with that guilt, and it's like living with a crazy person inside your head. It plays on your mind, goading you, tormenting you. I think that's probably why I drank so much. Most nights, come three a.m., I would be awake, driven half mad by a carousel of regret. Why didn't I tell her I loved her all the time? Why didn't I do more to show her how much I loved her? I'd thought I would have the rest of my life to make her my priority. Why had I taken that for granted? I could have done so much more, made her so much happier. My mind was a circle of guilt, going round and round – a never-ending roundabout of guilt.

My biggest regret that haunted my nights, and stole any hope of sleep, was that I had not let her talk to me about the fact that she was dying. All those weeks I wasted when she could have been telling me what to do – how to look after the children, how to care for them as they grew older. I've never known anyone more organised than Rebecca – she could have planned a military invasion if she'd put her mind to it. There was so much she could have put in place for her kids' future without her – and I didn't allow that to happen. I denied Rebecca her chance to do that, and robbed the children of all the love and care she could have left behind for them in those empty notepads. If I had been spared guilt for most of my life, it sure as hell was payback time now.

WHEN MY DAD was a young man, he used to worry about being anything remotely like his father. As he's grown older, he's looked back and seen he was more like his dad than he ever realised or wanted to be. Over the years Dad has managed to change, and for his daughters and grandchildren he's been a thousand times more open and loving than he was ever able to be when he lived with us. He has become a true grandfather to my kids, and that means the world to me. Someone asked him recently what the differences were between him and me. He thought about it, and couldn't come up with one. It's true: we're unbelievably similar. But I don't want to be the dad he was when I was young. I want to be a better dad. I want to be able to change, just like he could.

On those long, lonely nights in the house after Rebecca died, I thought a lot about how I had jumped to the wrong conclusions when my mum and dad split up. For years I was furious because they wouldn't talk to me about why they'd separated. I don't want my kids to feel in the dark like that, not knowing what's going on and unable to tell anyone how they feel. That is the last thing Rebecca would have wanted. The painful truth was that had they lost their dad and not their mum, she would have known how to give them the love and trust they needed to open up. She would have been able to help them.

My guilt about not showing Rebecca enough love when she was alive was agony enough. The thought that I might not show my kids enough love now that she was gone was more than I could bear. Was I going to keep repeating the same cycle of mistakes over and over? My dad was a better father than his. Now I had to be a better dad than mine had been. If Rebecca had not died I could probably have carried on as I was for the rest of my life. But I'd always said I would do anything for my children – and I meant it. Staring into the dark, night after night, in an empty bed, I now understood what I had to do. However much I hated the idea, I was going to have to ask for help.

But how? Who would I ask? The thought of going to see a therapist or counsellor made me feel sick. What could some professional who had never even known Rebecca tell me about how I felt at losing her? Letters after your name and textbooks on your shelf do not make you an expert on me and my family. I found the idea of a therapist a joke. Why would I want to go and sit in a room with a stranger who hadn't experienced what I was going through? In my mind, that would be like trying to learn to drive with an instructor who hadn't passed his own driving test.

When I was at Man United I did see a sports psychologist for a while. At first I'd been sceptical – but it really did help improve my game. In my mind, however, that was different. That was about helping me achieve a goal. That was about winning.

Looking back now, I can see I was probably being stubborn. My hostility to therapy was irrationally judgemental, and maybe I was just looking for excuses not to do something I found so difficult. But even then, deep down, I knew my emotional coldness – my total inability to talk about my feelings – went even further than Rebecca's death, and that its impact reached beyond my family. Bereavement was opening my eyes to all the other ways in which my way of thinking was a problem.

For example, I had always found gratitude practically impossible to express. It's not that I don't feel grateful to lots of people. I do, more than they could possibly imagine. But saying it, or showing it? That's another matter. The other day I sent my agent, Jamie, a text message about all the outstanding work he had been doing for me lately, and for once I actually thanked him. It wasn't the world's most profuse thank-you, not by a long way. But it was a thank-you.

Nice to get that text off you, mate, he messaged back. *Cos I don't really know whether you're ever happy about something or not.* I read his text twice, taken aback. Didn't he? It hadn't occurred to me that a thank-you was not something other people might merely like: they actually needed it.

Rebecca used to be brilliant at thank-you cards. She was always popping something in the post to someone – a little note or a gift – and I know how much it meant to the recipients. So now I knew I should be saying, 'Thank you,' to Sandra. Sandra is in her sixties, and would probably rather be retired by now, but instead she dropped everything to leave Manchester and come south and move in with us. She left her life behind for us, and where we would be without her I don't even like to think.

After she had been with us for a while, she decided to take up walking. Watching her set off from the house one afternoon, an idea came to me: why not get Sandra some trainers? So I went out and bought her a wicked pair.

But could I give them to her? I felt sick with embarrassment, just thinking about it. What would I say? How would I do it? I know, I thought, I'll just leave them by her bed. But what about when she finds them? She's bound to come and give me a cuddle or something, and I won't know what to say. It isn't as if we don't give each other a kiss on the cheek most days; that's not the problem. It's the awkwardness of gratitude that makes me want the earth to open and swallow me.

Remember, I'm not talking about people I don't know very well. I'm talking about one of my best mates and agent, and the woman who lives with us and knows me inside out. If it felt unnatural to say, 'Thank you,' even to them, I knew I was in trouble.

And I really was in trouble. Night after night, despair was eating me up. Was my smile going to be fake for the rest of my life? I couldn't see any possibility of ever feeling happy again, so, yes, it probably was. I would have to put a plastic public grin on my face for ever. I was never going to laugh genuinely again. It would only ever be the tinny, forced noise I found myself making whenever I was expected to appear amused. I would never enjoy the ordinary pleasures of family life, like going to the shops or taking the kids to a restaurant. I could still go out with my mates, and have what I used to think of as a good night out – but where would be the point? What good would it do? I was only ever happy going out because I knew I'd be coming home to Rebecca. Without her, I would never, ever enjoy anything again.

Even if I could, guilt would instantly destroy it. How could I think about enjoying myself when Rebecca lay in a grave? In the unlikely event that anything ever looked like it might bring me happiness, even for a second, I would look at my children growing up without a mother and that moment would be stolen. We could plan a perfect family day, play frisbee in the park, see a movie, go for pizza and ice cream – but the better the day, the worse I felt. Any glimmer of joy – even seeing the kids open their stockings on Christmas morning – was always corrupted by her absence. When the price for a second of pleasure with my children was the pain of knowing she had been denied it, where was the point in even trying? I couldn't savour the pride of watching my boys play football when all I could think was, Rebecca should be here on the touchline beside me, cheering them on.

Somehow we stumbled through the kids' first birthdays without her, our first Christmas and the first anniversary of her death. On each occasion the whole family would gather together, at our house or in a pub or restaurant for a meal, but no matter how many people sat around the table or how much noise we made, the deafening silence and absence of Rebecca was all I could feel.

And then there was the bleak, bitter loneliness, which went way beyond merely missing Rebecca or searching for her in my sleep. It was the loneliness of pretending to the world that I was still a normal person – that I was all right – when inside I was broken. People saw me on the school run, they saw me on the television, and because I wasn't in tears they assumed I must be okay. They did not see that twenty times a day I was doubled up inside, scarcely able to breathe.

This could not go on. This could not be the man my kids' dad had become. My children had already lost their mother. They couldn't lose the person their father used to be, too, and be left with this shell of a wreck.

WHEN THE IDEA of making a documentary about learning to grieve first came up, I was doubtful. It was about six months after Rebecca had died – and I felt self-conscious enough about asking for help as it was. Doing it on camera did not sound to me like a strategy that would make the ordeal any easier.

It was Jamie's idea in the beginning. Some football agents regard their role as strictly commercial: their job is to maximise their clients' earnings, and nothing more. But Jamie's always understood that I have other ambitions for my profile beyond merely making money, and it's one of the reasons why I think we have always worked so well together.

I was still playing professional football when I set up the Rio Ferdinand Foundation, to support youngsters from deprived inner-city backgrounds like mine, and its work means as much – maybe more – to me as anything else I do today. When you come from a council estate in Peckham, it doesn't matter how much money you have in the bank. You know how hard other people's lives are, and if you've got anything about you at all, if you can do something to help then you should.

Since Rebecca had died, Jamie had witnessed at close hand the terrible state I was in. He knew I needed to get help – and knew me well enough to understand what a challenge that was going to be. But Jamie could also see – long before it dawned on me – that we could use my profile to share this help with other men who found themselves in a similar boat to me. By making a documentary about learning how to grieve, I would not just be helping myself, but maybe many others too.

At that point I was still too lost in my own grief to be able to grasp this. What persuaded me to make the film was the indisputable logic of Jamie's argument that, if I was serious about wanting to change, I was going to have to ask for help one way or another – and having signed up for the documentary, I'd be obliged to see it through. If I got cold feet – and I almost certainly would – the option of changing my mind and pulling out would no longer be available. I decided to think of the cameras as the equivalent of a personal trainer. We all want to get fit, but there are days when getting to the gym and pushing our body to the limit feels beyond us. A personal trainer's job is to make sure we do, whether we feel like it or not – and the cameras could perform the same function.

I knew which professional I wanted to approach first. He was the only one I trusted beyond all doubt, and who I knew had the answers I needed. Professor Stephen Johnson is a consultant oncologist at the Royal Marsden, and had been Rebecca's doctor. He was by our side through the darkest horrors, and understood what I had lived through. Even more importantly, he understood exactly what Rebecca had died from.

This is highly embarrassing to have to admit, and I wish it was not true, but up until this point, had anyone asked me how Rebecca had died, I honestly could not have told them. I knew she'd had breast cancer when we lived in Manchester, but what had happened to her body eighteen months later and what had taken her life were a blank mystery. During all those meetings in the Royal Marsden with Mr Johnson and his team, while they were explaining scan results, blood tests, treatment options, drug trials, I had given every appearance of listening closely and taking in what I was told. In reality, they might as well have been speaking in Russian.

How could I begin to grieve for a life when I didn't even understand how or why it had been lost? I invited Mr Johnson to our house to explain, and with great kindness he agreed. Perhaps he had guessed all along that I'd been processing nothing during those dark weeks in hospital – or maybe it was just that he had heard the same thing so many times from families of patients. Relatives do try to follow what he tells them, but it's as if their love for the patient he is trying to save drowns his words. We cannot hear him.

Listening to him explain now what had happened to Rebecca, it was as if I was hearing it for the first time. He described how the original tumour had metastasised not only to her bones, which they might have been able to treat, but to her bone marrow, which had made her condition much more serious. It was viciously aggressive, and spread to her liver, causing the organ to bleed and fail.

Did I want to know all of this? No, of course I didn't. But I no longer wanted *not* to know it. One day my children would need answers – and when that time came, I would now be able to give them. Ignorance is not always bliss. In my case, it was just denial in disguise.

Here are some things I have learned

- *Take a friend*

If someone close to you is very ill, you'll probably want to go with them to all their medical appointments. You'll want to understand the treatment options. But even if you would normally consider yourself quite capable of processing complex information, don't assume you will be in this situation.

Don't underestimate what fear can do to your brain's ability to function. Don't expect yourself to absorb what the doctors tell you. Even the most intelligent people forget great chunks of it within minutes of leaving the consulting room. This is very common, and totally normal.

Ask someone else to come with you to every appointment, to listen and take notes and, if necessary, ask questions. Choose someone you feel is close enough to trust, but not so close that their own feelings run the risk of hijacking their concentration. Their job is to help you, not to get upset themselves.

- *Let a loved one talk about dying if they want to*

We have all been told how important it is to stay positive when someone's seriously ill, especially if it's cancer. We have heard of the miraculous recoveries that leave doctors dumbfounded, and can only be put down to the power of positive thinking. We've heard, too, the tales of patients who seem to sabotage their own treatment by refusing to believe it might work.

What I didn't know, though, until long after Rebecca died, is that those who confront their mortality head on, and can talk about their death, stand a much better chance of coming to terms with the end of their life, and being able to face it with peace.

If someone you love is dying and wants to confront it and talk about it, try not to stop them. How they spend the time they have left is their prerogative to decide, and if they want to spell out their plans and wishes for a future they won't see, let them, and try to really listen. I will never forgive myself for stopping Rebecca talking about it, and would give anything now for what she could have told me about how to help the children when she was gone.

When you're sitting at your loved one's deathbed it might feel cruel, or dangerous, or simply too upsetting, to let them talk about dying. But, trust me, it is the most loving thing you can do.

• *Guilt is normal and natural, but it is not your friend.*
Grief is the number-one emotion we associate with death, but the bereaved are almost as likely to experience guilt as well. Some of us will suffer from survivors' guilt, others blame themselves for the death, and many feel guilty for even trying to find any pleasure in their future.

So, guilt is natural. It is not, however, helpful. Studies have found that people who suffer higher levels of guilt often find it hard to grieve and express their sadness, and other studies have found that the guiltier you feel, the longer you will take to come to terms with your loss and recover.

There is no magic formula to make guilt vanish, but one trick I've found helpful is worth a try. When you talk to yourself, pretend you're talking to a friend you care about. This friend has gone through everything you have been through; their circumstances are identical to yours. The only difference is that this friend is not you but someone else.

Would you accuse them of all the sins and crimes and failures you lay on yourself? Would you punish them with scorn and contempt? Or would you feel nothing but compassion and sympathy for their situation, and respect for their resilience?

Give it a go and see for yourself. That guilty voice in your head? Stop listening to it. Ignore it. You wouldn't poison anyone else with its lies, so don't let it get to you.

• *You won't feel this way forever*
As if grief wasn't bad enough in itself, what makes it so much worse is the impossibility of imagining it will ever ease. You believe you will go on feeling as terrible as this forever. When Rebecca died, the idea that one day I might begin to feel better would have struck me as laughable, and when people promised me I would, I assumed they were trying to trick me into false hope. I thought I was too smart to fall for that. In fact, I wasn't smart enough to see that what had actually deceived me wasn't false hope but false despair.

The bereaved are particularly susceptible to what psychologists call 'permanence' thinking. It's a classic symptom of depression, and can keep us trapped in our unhappiness. When someone is convinced they will never be happy, it can become a self-fulfilling prophecy.

I know how persuasive this kind of permanence thinking can be. I know, too, that anyone locked in its grip will laugh if I promise them that their pain will one day ease. It will. Of course it will. But I know better than to expect anyone to believe me.

Instead, I'd suggest trying this. Rather than say you 'always' feel miserable, try saying 'sometimes'. When anyone asks how you are, try telling them how you feel *today*. If you find yourself thinking, I can *never* be happy, write it down. Then think of any tiny moments of happiness you've had – playing with your kids, watching the sunset, laughing at the TV – and write them down. I bet you'll be surprised by how much you can write. Now reread your statement that you can 'never' be happy, and ask yourself if it's really true.

CHAPTER ELEVEN

Opening Up

IT'S A COLD grey afternoon in late 2016. I'm on a flight home
from Belfast to London. It's one of those funny little planes
that feel more like gliders than jets, and seem so flimsy you
wonder how they even get off the ground. We're crossing
the Irish Sea now, and have just run into some serious turbulence. The plane is bouncing about like a mule. It's a
commuter flight, full of mostly businessmen, and their eyes
have been buried in the *Financial Times*, but even they start
to look up and wonder whether overhead lockers are about
to start flying open.

I'm a good flier, but I do not love turbulence, and this is
not your average bumpy patch. This is something else. Under
normal circumstances, by now I'd be tightening my grip on
the armrest. My knuckles would be white. But today? Today
I couldn't care less. I have a smile on my face that stretches
from one ear to the other, and it's been there ever since I
set off for the airport. It would take more than turbulence
to wipe this smile off my face.

This isn't the fake plastic grin I put on in public to make

other people happy. This smile glows from inside me. This smile is real.

WHEN YOU'RE THIRTY-SIX years old, you don't know many other widowers, and certainly none of your own age. I was still at that stage in life when you're going to more weddings than funerals, and some of my friends hadn't even settled down. No one I knew had lost his wife, and there were days when I felt like a freak. One of Rebecca's best friends got married just weeks after she died, and at the wedding it felt as if everywhere I turned all I could see were couples.

In those early weeks, just getting through each day seemed like a miracle. The simplest daily task could feel like a life-and-death battle. In the months that followed, though, daily life began to feel less like mortal combat and more like an unending war of attrition – and, in some ways, that was worse. There were mornings when I woke up feeling equal to the world, and would begin to hope the worst was behind me. But the very next day it was as if the clouds had darkened again, and even getting out of bed was beyond me. As I cancelled the day's plans, and curled up in a ball beneath the duvet, I wondered if I was going to feel this way forever. More than anything, what I wanted was to meet other widowed dads like me.

The documentary team suggested Ben Brooks-Dutton. In November 2012, Ben was strolling through West Hampstead with his wife, Desreen, and their two-year-old son, Jackson, when a passing driver lost control at the wheel and ploughed onto the pavement. Desreen was killed instantly. They had married only the previous year, and were a mixed-race couple. She was black, he was white, and both were just thirty-three. In the blink of an eye, Ben had gone from being one half of a happy couple to a single dad and widower. If anyone knew how I was feeling, and could tell me what to expect, it was Ben.

Since Desreen had died, Ben had been writing a blog about his life as a young widowed father. Through this he had formed a support group of other men in the same boat. They met fairly regularly, often at one of their homes, to eat together and chat about what was going on. Sometimes they would go away for weekends with their kids. They were all just normal, ordinary blokes who had got horribly unlucky.

Ben and the team exchanged emails. I was far from the first shattered new widower to approach him, and he had a suggestion to make. Would I like to come and meet a group of some widowed dads?

Yes. No. Probably. Maybe not. To be honest, for someone like me to walk into a house full of strangers and have a conversation about feelings was more daunting than any cup final I had ever played in. Would it be like AA, where we would all sit in a circle and I'd have to say, 'My name's Rio and I'm a widowed dad'?

No, Ben reassured me. I think he was quite amused. 'It's nothing like that at all. Everyone brings food and beer, and we sit around chatting, just like we would in the pub.'

'Okay, then, you're on. Count me in.'

I didn't think much about how it would feel for the other widowers to have me showing up. I was too busy with my own nerves. Ben had told me to bring food, so I made macaroni cheese. Was that the right sort of thing? And what should I wear? When the day came I told myself to stop being so stupid. This was my first chance to meet men who could actually give me more than sympathy and kindly stares. Shut up with your fretting, Rio, I told myself. Just get in the car.

At the house there were five guys, all roughly my kind of age. There were firm handshakes all round, and for the first few minutes we did that slightly awkward blokey thing of standing around with folded arms, but soon we were all sitting round a big wooden dining table looking out onto the garden. Ben fired up the barbecue, beers were opened, and if anyone had wandered in off the street they would have thought this was a bunch of mates hanging out for the afternoon.

Ben got us going, and talked a bit about the question all of us had had to face. 'How are you supposed to grieve like a man when you don't even know what it is to grieve?'

Another guy said his son had told him recently, 'I don't want to cry because men don't cry.'

Ben grinned and nodded. 'It seems to be all right to cry at football matches but you're not supposed to cry when your wife dies. How can that be?'

Alistair, the one whose son had said men don't cry, spread his arms as if to say, Crazy, isn't it? He was the most recently bereaved, after his wife, Andrea, had lost a long battle with cancer. 'Sometimes,' he said, 'I put a pair of Andrea's socks on, I light the candles, stick on one of her films and I have a cry.'

I wanted to hear all their stories. Another guy, Dan, joked, 'This is like the worst game of Top Trumps.' Dan's wife was run over on a pelican crossing in 2012, leaving him widowed with a two-year-old son. But it got worse. In 2015 he had had a daughter with his new partner – but the baby girl had spent five and a half months in intensive care and had died over the Christmas just gone. The doctors had broken the news to Dan that his daughter wasn't going to make it on the third anniversary of his wife's death.

The tragedies they were describing chilled my veins, but they all talked openly, and I didn't feel awkward at all as I listened. Alistair's words about wearing his wife's socks had made me smile; he was a big, tough-looking bloke with a shaven head. Fair play to him, I thought. It takes some man to share something as private as that without any embarrassment. I was full of admiration and respect.

But it was Dan who had me spellbound. To have lost his wife, and then his child, was to be cursed beyond my comprehension. I couldn't stop staring at him. How could he just sit there like that, telling his story, so calm and strong? I kept looking him up and down, searching for cracks. He should have been a broken man. How did he keep going? If that had been me, I was certain I would have fallen to pieces. But, then, before it had happened to Dan, he probably would have thought the same. I was starting to see what the human spirit is capable of withstanding when it has to, and it went beyond anything I would have believed possible. I had imagined that meeting these guys would be informative – maybe even comforting. I had not guessed they would be inspiring.

The more I watched and listened, the more I began to realise: This is what real grieving looks like. These men seemed so sorted and together, as if each one had a map inside his mind and knew where he was going. They all acknowledged that there were still dark moments when they felt lost. But whereas my map looked like Spaghetti Junction, and most days I didn't know whether to turn left or right, these widowers were on the right track.

It wasn't hard to work out why. The difference between them and me was obvious. They had grieved, and so could see light at the end of the tunnel. I hadn't, and that was why I couldn't. Looking back now, I can of course see that grief isn't some sort of competition; there is no magic winning formula, and everyone grieves in their own way. But that day I saw what progress could look like.

I can remember only one other occasion in my adult life when I had been surrounded by a group of men who made me feel inadequate about my own progress. On my very first day at Man United I walked into the dressing room, looked around me and thought, Oh, my God. He's got three trophies, he's got four Premier League titles, he's got six, he's got five. And me? I've got zero. I need to do some work.

But the biggest shock of all that day was the conversation about wedding rings. At one point or another after losing their wives, these widowers had stopped wearing their rings.

I couldn't believe it. How could they do that? Until now the idea of removing mine hadn't even crossed my mind – and now that it had, it made me dizzy. If these guys had not been sitting right in front of me, talking openly about their heartbreak, I would have said that any man who stops wearing his wedding ring after his wife dies must be one heartless bastard. Either that, or his marriage had been a joke.

It's amazing how easy it is to be judgemental when you don't know what you're talking about, isn't it? Before Rebecca died, if we had been watching TV and seen a widower begin dating again within five years of losing his wife, we would have looked at each other and said the same thing. 'Well, that just shows he never really loved her, doesn't it?' We wouldn't have thought twice about it.

But sitting there now, I began to see how ignorant we all are about a situation until it happens to us. These men were not callous, and they had not been hasty. They were grown men facing up to bitter reality, then finding the courage to deal with it and move on. I felt nothing but shame for my old self, so unqualified to judge yet so quick to do so. After meeting these men I wouldn't judge another widower if he started dating the day after burying his wife. Until you have walked in these shoes, you do not have a clue.

I came away so affected by Dan's story that a few weeks later I travelled up to Warrington to visit him and his partner, Anna, and his six-year-old son, Jamie. After playing football in the garden with Jamie, I sat down to talk with Anna and Dan.

'How can you tell,' I wanted to know, 'when it's a good moment to talk to Jamie about his mum? How do you know when to bring her up?' From their gentle expressions I suspected they wondered if I might be fixating on finding the right time as a way of delaying it. Maybe they were right.

Anna had lost her daughter only six months earlier, yet she seemed more concerned for me than for herself. That shook me a bit. She talked about the temptation to throw oneself into work, and the illusion that grief can somehow be short-circuited with a busy enough diary, and as she talked I began to understand what she meant. As I drove home that night, two things this incredible couple had told me were ringing in my ears.

'To focus too much on work is probably detrimental in the long term,' Anna had said softly. 'And I worry a bit about that for you.'

'Life is short,' Dan said – and God knows he should know. 'Grab it by the balls. Keep working at being alive.'

THE WIDOWERS I met have all suffered terrible heartbreak, and each one has found different tools and strategies to deal with his grief. I felt incredibly lucky to have had this oppor-tunity to talk with them. For anyone reading this who may be suffering with their own loss, I hope it will be helpful to hear some of their stories in their own words.

Dave

I met my fiancée Sam in mid-2004. In April 2005 she found a lump in her breast and was diagnosed with breast cancer. She was basically having treatment for all the time we were together, for seven years. She died in 2012, about three and a half weeks before we could get married. She fought it – went on all the clinical trials – but it was just prolonging her life, not saving her life. In the end it spread to her brain, and she went into a hospice after her sister couldn't wake her at home. She died a week later.

There were some issues resulting from Sam's past that had to be resolved first. So we went to court for six months to sort that out, and I kind of put my grief on hold. At the end of it I had a complete meltdown. I phoned up the hospital and said, 'I need to talk to someone. My head is about to explode. I don't know if I'm coming or going.' So I did seek out counselling. When Sam first died I was like, 'It's not for me. I don't need to talk to anyone. I'll be absolutely fine.' And it was probably the best thing I ever did, actually seeking help. I get that it's not for everyone. But I'm a big advocate for it – if you find the right one, it's amazing. It does wonders.

When people offer to help you, take them up on it. There are going to be people who say, 'If there's anything I can do, give me a shout', and you'll probably find that eighty per cent of that is just lip service. But you'll get people who will genuinely offer to come round and cook you a dinner so you haven't got to, or do your washing or ironing. So just take that help. I never did, and it's the biggest mistake I ever made. I drove myself to exhaustion. I did the typical thing of trying to tough it out, saying, 'I don't need anyone. I'm a big tough guy. I'll crack on and do it on my own.'

My girlfriend now is a widow. Because she'd had a similar experience, we kind of got talking about that. I'd got to the point where I wasn't consciously looking, but I'd kind of got used to being on my own. So it came out of the blue. I felt very guilty about it. But Sam always said to me, 'If there's such things as ghosts, if you don't get out there and meet someone I'm going to come back and haunt the shit out of you.' It was just over four years before I started dating again, but I don't think you can put a time scale on it. You need to do what's right for you.

Alistair

Andrea died in March 2016. She had non-smoker's lung cancer – she was diagnosed on Valentine's Day 2011. Our son Archie is now eight. Although the diagnosis was five years before she died, it still came around quicker than we expected. Andrea left some voice messages for Archie and we made sure we took lots of pictures and tried to create as many memories beforehand as possible, but it's pretty tough watching someone you love go through so much pain and slowly fade away.

On the eighth of every month, because Andrea was born on 8 March, we have Andrea's Day or Mummy's Day. So we do something she would have liked to do, even just having a coffee, because she liked a coffee, and just remember her. Because no one remembers when they're eight years old, really – he needs reminding of things constantly. I think we'll keep doing it for ever. Archie is very much like me: he doesn't want to be sad. If I say, 'Let's get Mummy's pictures out', he'll say, 'I don't want to see them because seeing them will make me sad.' It's just a constant battle with your own demons trying to figure out what is the best thing to do for them. So we always talk about Andrea in a positive way.

You can get a bit cut off from friends. For one reason or another people struggle to communicate with people who have lost someone they love. I just wanted to talk to someone who had been through a similar thing, because they would understand a bit more. People said to me, 'Go and see a counsellor', but I just didn't find it helped me. They weren't going to bring Andrea back, they weren't going to make my life any easier, and I always said I wanted to find a support group, and then I found one online.

The best piece of advice I was given was that there is no need to be strong. If I could go back to me at the time that Andrea died, I would tell myself not to stress about things that don't matter, and that I'll be all right. Because I am all right now. I do feel guilty, because I read about people years on who are still having days from hell, and I think, Why don't I feel like that? Did I not really love her? Did I not really care about her? But you can't change how you feel. I don't not think about her any more: I just deal with it in a different way. My favourite saying that comes from it all is 'Don't wait for the storm to pass – learn how to dance in the rain.' And me and Andrea had had that saying from before she died. Although it was raining all around us, we were just trying to make the best of every moment.

Martin

I lost my wife Jayne in November 2013. She'd been diagnosed about a year and a half earlier with cancer. She'd been ill for probably nine months – she'd been going to the doctor and she'd had stomach pains, and they basically came to the conclusion that she had irritable bowel syndrome. They put her on medication for that, but two months later there was no change. She ended up going and getting further tests, and they realised she had colorectal cancer. It was so advanced at that point that there was no way back from it. It was a question of how long. She went through a bout of chemotherapy and they said, 'We think there's a possibility here that we could have real life extension', and we saw some specialists about the possibility of cutting some of her liver away. But then they said, 'No, that's not on the table any more.' We went through grief then, when the doctor told us what was wrong, that it was terminal.

It's up and down all the time, but that mimics the way grief works. I'm three and a half years in now, and I still have up and down days. The difference is that the downs aren't as long, and I can control them to an extent, whereas at first they were all-consuming and I couldn't get out of bed for six months.

About six weeks after she died I saw a grief counsellor. I sat there, and I spoke, and I listened, and I thought, This is a complete waste of time. And then after about two and a half years, I went back to somebody. It felt better. It was a lot easier. It worked for me. I just think I wasn't ready to open up when I first went. I hadn't processed it myself. A counsellor can't tell you how to feel, they just help you get your feelings out.

You need to take the time to understand how your world is because your world totally changes. As a guy, with a nine-to-five job, wife at home with the kids, your responsibilities are bringing the money home, keeping the roof over their heads, and then you come home and spend a bit of time with the kids and then the kids go to bed, and you spend all weekend going out as a family. And that totally changes when your wife dies. The emotional welfare of the children becomes your priority. I think you've got to find a silver lining to every dark cloud. And for me, the silver lining to losing Jayne is that I've now got a closeness with my kids that a lot of fathers don't have.

Dan

My wife Helen was killed the week before Christmas in 2012. Helen went to work in the morning, she went out at lunchtime to get gifts for our nieces, and on the way back from Toys R Us she stopped at a pelican crossing to cross a dual carriageway. There were two lanes of cars – there was a white van stopped in the first lane, and as she passed the white van a car came through the red light. It knocked her off her feet and smashed her on the floor. She never woke up.

Me and Helen met in 2006. We went on a night out in Manchester with the man who would end up my best man. He was mates with Helen at university, so we all met up. We got together that night and were together ever since, pretty much. I was twenty-eight, I proposed when I was twenty-nine and we got married in 2008. We had a little boy, Jamie, in 2010.

I found at the beginning that telling people about it helped to normalise it for me. So I've told the story of what went on lots and lots of times. Over time it got less painful and less unreal. I talk about Helen with Jamie all the time. He's got pictures, and he talks about her an awful lot. There's pictures all through the house, and we've got videos. I found the wedding video the other week, which is a bit spooky. I watched it, and it set me off a bit – I haven't heard Helen speak since 2012. It was the first time I've ever watched the wedding video.

I'm not very good at seeking help, to be fair. I know a lot of guys who have got help, counselling and tablets. The first thing I did do, though, was hide all the alcohol in the house because I had a two-year-old to look after. Not that I had the urge, but I just wanted to get rid of it before I had the urge. I spent a few days changing around the whole of the bedroom. It's not mine and Helen's bedroom any more, it's my bedroom and my playtime space with Jamie. And changing that around was quite therapeutic to me. I'm an engineer: I get on well when I've got things to do and problems to solve.

Jamie was asking why he didn't have a mummy, so I decided I needed to bring someone into the family, not just for me but for Jamie as well. I met Anna on eHarmony. We got on really well, and I introduced her to Jamie and he really liked her. So Anna and I had a big long discussion about marriage and kids, and we decided that, yes, that's what we wanted to do. And we just made a decision between the two of us, as we were getting close to forty and it gets harder to have kids the older you get, so we decided to do that first, have ourselves a little page boy or a little flower girl and get married further down the line.

It took us a while to get Scarlett. When we went for the second scan, they told us that she wasn't growing enough, that she was too small, so we knew there were going to be issues. She was C-sectioned at thirty weeks, and she was just over a kilo. And she was beautiful, she was laughing from the get-go. But her insides weren't working properly, she had all sorts of problems, and in the end, five and a half months later after living in the hospital every day, we had to say goodbye. We took her off all the machines. She lived for about twenty-four hours. She was in Anna's arms, just closed her eyes and went to sleep.

There's a fair amount of shielding the person you're speaking to about the story. Quite often I can just drop people like a stone, just by accident. Quite a lot of life can become not telling people the whole truth. One of the things a lot of people – family and friends and stuff – didn't get was every day that I woke up, as soon as I opened my eyes in the morning, the first fraction of the second was 'Where is my wife?' Then your brain goes, 'She's not here any more.' From as soon as you do that, all that time till you close your eyes and go to sleep, you're living that process where your wife is missing. A whole chunk of you is missing. We had been two pieces of one whole, and half of that disappeared overnight.

I don't think I'd change anything that I did, looking back. What I discovered is, there are no wrong answers, there are just answers. It was just something I had to get through. There are positive things that come out of bad times. You can't pity yourself all the time and say, 'Oh, woe is me.' You've got to step up and stand up to it.

Tim

My wife Natalie passed away on 3 July 2014. Her body shut down two minutes after giving birth. She died from a rare condition called amniotic fluid embolism. So I left the hospital with a newborn baby and our three-year-old son.

I remember, coming back from the hospital, I had gone

into what I can only describe as deep shock. A lot of the staff at the hospital were not able to deal with the situation – they're trained to deliver babies. What happened to my wife happens something like once in every ten years. I didn't know for a long time what had happened to her – it was a couple of months.

I went three or four days after my wife died to see a grief counsellor, who first said to me that people in the same situation very, very slowly manage to rebuild their lives. At that stage I was so full of shock and disbelief I couldn't even begin to think about a future ahead. But I would recommend it – go and see a grief counsellor. Mine gave me professional feedback on what would happen to me in that time. She was the one who told me that when everything is too much for you, you just shut down. It would help me understand what was happening to my body and my mind. It gives you more of a sense of control.

It's hard to really convey, but it was such a big deal for me to get in touch with the Facebook group. I don't know how I would have found the kind of support that I needed personally, which was to be in touch with other men who I could relate to. The trouble being a young man, there aren't that many groups out there.

It's very hard to speak about Natalie with my kids. I think I could have done a better job but I just find it so hard, so painful. I think the best advice I got was that you have to be one hundred per cent honest and truthful. You can't dress it up, because they'll figure out the truth for themselves anyway. The hardest part is that you have to repeat yourself over and over again. My grief counsellor helped me see that it's kind of tough love. You have to be able to say, 'This is the situation. Nothing will bring back Natalie. This is how it is.' My daughter is three now and doesn't know yet, but she calls for her mum all the time. It's heartbreaking. It's totally different because her birth is so interlinked with her mother's death, so it's difficult because she's got all of that to come.

Practical things always help. Exercise, running, doing something to burn off all your energy – that's really, really important. I got told once to write everything that needs to be done on Post-it notes and stick them on the fridge. Like, mow the lawn, clean the bath, wash the dishes. So then, when you get people saying that really clichéd thing of 'If there's anything I can do to help', you've got something to give them.

It's always good to have someone help you get things done, like closing down your wife's bank accounts, probate, being able to stop all the mail coming to your wife. There are loads of things that you have to do. One of the hardest parts is that there's no one really there telling you what you should and shouldn't do, and it's overwhelming. I think the hardest part of it is that there is no instruction manual for how to get through it.

There was one other widower the documentary team suggested I meet: Darren Clarke. I didn't have to think twice. Darren Clarke has always been one of my heroes – a world-class golfer from Northern Ireland, who won the British Open in 2011. He was always one of the most popular players on the circuit, and in 2006 everyone's heart broke for him when

187

his wife died of breast cancer at the Royal Marsden, leaving behind two young sons for him to raise alone. Just six weeks later he represented his country in the Ryder Cup, and won. Along with everyone else, I was bowled over by his bravery and grace. Did I want to meet him? Of course I did.

But no amount of admiration could have prepared me for the impact of meeting Darren. Looking back now, I realise I was at a very low ebb. The initial shock and disbelief had functioned almost as an anaesthetic in the early months of my widowhood, and I think that back then the future had felt like an abstract concept. Just getting through each day had been enough of a challenge. But as the months passed, and one milestone after another had been faced – the first birthdays, Christmas, the anniversary of her death – the horrifying permanence of loss had slowly begun to sink in. It was hard to believe we could survive the first year – but when we did, the only reward was the terrible reality that we would have to survive another, and another, and another.

If I'm being completely honest, by the time I set off to meet Darren I was getting a bit weary of friends and family promising me I would be happy again one day. 'Rio,' they would urge, with forced smiles and big eyes full of concern, 'Life's going to get better, I just know it is.' How did they know? They couldn't possibly know. All I could hear was a loved one desperately worried for me, making a well-meant but to my ears meaningless attempt to cheer me up.

Had the tables been turned, I know I would have said the same to them. What I couldn't have known was how little it would help. But when Darren told me, 'Listen to me, Rio. You will be happy,' it was like the sun coming out from behind the clouds.

We met in the lounge of the Europa Hotel in Belfast city centre. I'd stayed there before, when playing away against Northern Ireland for England. This time we sat at a little round table in the window drinking coffee. Darren is ten years older than me, and had been widowed for a decade, but the parallels between our stories were almost uncanny. The big difference was in our demeanours. I looked tense and tired – my default expression in those days – whereas Darren twinkled with charm and Irish good cheer.

'I never thought this would happen.' He beamed. 'I didn't

With Darren Clarke

think I would ever be this happy again. But, look, I'm as happy now as I have ever been.' He was almost laughing as he said it, and I knew it was true. Therapists can study the science of grief until it's coming out of their ears, but they can ultimately only promise you a theory. Darren actually knew what he was talking about – and because of that, I believed him.

What he said next struck me with even greater force. 'And, Rio, don't try and stop it.'

I didn't need to ask him what he meant. One of the worst things about grief is the endless conflict you wrestle with every day. Half of you longs to feel better – and the other half thinks if you did, you would be letting down your lost loved one. Darren knows this as well as any man, because in 2012 he had remarried and was blissfully happy with his second wife.

'I know you worry about being disloyal,' Darren went on, as if reading my mind. 'I know you do. It's completely natural. But, my friend, Rebecca would not want you to be miserable for the rest of your life. Life has to go on – and there is life out there afterwards. And if you don't believe me when I say that, you know you can't argue with what I'm about to say next. In the long run, your kids will only get through this if they see you smiling again. If you love your kids – and I know you do – you need to do it for them.'

There aren't many moments in life that you can honestly say made you a different man. But the person who flew home from Belfast that day was not the same man who had flown out a day earlier. Something profound had changed.

Darren had given me something I hadn't thought I believed in any more. He had given me hope. I couldn't stop smiling on that plane home because, for the first time, I was starting to think I might – just might – one day be happy again.

Here are some things I have learned

• *Find a local or online support group and meet other people in the same shoes*

Men aren't good at asking for help. More than 85 per cent of the people who seek grief support after the loss of a child, parent or partner are women; men typically do what I did instead, and try to outrun, out-numb or out-busy their way around grief. It doesn't work. Men who repress or deny their grief are prone to long-term problems like depression and anxiety, and are even more likely to suffer physical symptoms like fatigue and backache too.

What does work is meeting other men who are also grieving. Most men who join groups report a dramatic improvement in their state of mind, and there is an amazing amount of support out there if you look. Many of the widowers I met said that joining a Facebook group was the single most helpful thing they did. I've listed some of the groups and organisations you might want to try in Where to Find Help (pages 259–61).

• *There is nothing wrong with dating again*

It is very, very common for widowers to remarry – and quickly. Most studies find that the average time between the death of a first wife and a second marriage is just two and a half years. The younger a widower is, the sooner he is likely to start dating and marry again.

Women tend to remarry less than men. Some studies have found that widowers are as much as ten times more likely to remarry than widows – and this may help to explain why women can often feel more critical than men towards a widower who starts dating again.

Grief can make you very vulnerable, and to feel judged when you're already so low can be unnerving. But try to remember this. No one, but no one, can tell you when it's the right time to date again. Only you can know. Have faith in your instincts, and don't let anyone make you feel guilty.

And if dating is the last thing on your mind, that's fine too. Feel no pressure to rush into anything before you're ready. Don't forget, the only person who can tell you if or when to date is you.

CHAPTER TWELVE

Remembering Mummy

IT IS LATE autumn 2016. I'm in bed at home. It has gone midnight, but I can't sleep. I turn to look at the body sleeping beside me, and in the darkness I smile at her. Tia is a very determined little girl, and ever since her mum died she has decided to make my bed hers. She's a shocking wriggler and kicker and, given half a chance, will starfish right in the middle, diagonally for good measure, leaving me just a triangle of sheet near the edge of the bed.

Sooner or later I know I'm going to have to talk Tia into going back to sleeping in her own bed. But not yet. The truth is, I probably need this as much as she does.

MAYBE IT WAS all down to meeting Darren Clarke. Maybe the simple fact of making the documentary was starting to shift something in my mind. But, for whatever reason, I was feeling ready to talk to some experts about grief. The documentary team got in touch with an organisation called Jigsaw South East, which offers bereavement counselling to

families like ours, and one morning two women from the charity came to the house to tell me about what exactly it is they do.

I don't know what I'd pictured in the past when I'd tried to imagine a grief counsellor, but it probably wasn't this pair. Sarah Muir and Nickey Price weren't preachy or pious, or pretending to have all the answers. They were just ordinary women, who in another life could quite easily have been friends of my mum or Rebecca's. And, for all my prejudices, what they had to say made a lot of sense.

'I think very often we have an expectation that we get over grief very quickly,' Sarah said. 'And I think all of the families who come to our groups would say that isn't the case. It can take years. But I think as a society we have an expectation that people will get over it.'

It can be as long as five years after a parent's death before a child feels ready to take part in one of the groups Jigsaw South East runs for bereaved families. There was no rush, Sarah and Nickey reassured me. Every family is different, and needs to take its own time.

Were my kids ready for something like this, I wondered? I had a feeling they might be. The person who probably still wasn't, if I was being completely honest, was me.

After meeting Sarah and Nickey I began to read a bit about bereavement counselling, and the kinds of things grief therapists recommend. If I had to sum it all up in a nutshell, it would go like this. When someone you love dies, there is no such thing as talking too much. You can never talk enough. The more children are involved in conversations about death, the less it will frighten them and the better they will cope.

It was a relief to see we had got a lot of things right about Rebecca's funeral. Bereavement counsellors are very big on making sure that children are included in as much as possible of what happens on the day. The biggest mistake they say people make is to think it will be too upsetting for kids, and keep them away, when in fact the opposite is true. The whole point of a funeral is to help everyone come to terms with what has happened, and nobody needs that more than the kids.

Grief therapists also talk a lot about the importance of small things. Death is such a massive thing that adults often imagine kids will need equally grand-scale solutions to get them through it, when really what children need doesn't have to be elaborate at all. Finding one-on-one time for them is hard when you're a single parent, but it means the world to a child to have your undivided attention.

All this rang true to me. But I didn't agree with everything I read. Most bereavement experts seem to think that when a parent is terminally ill, their children should be told the full truth, to help prepare them for the death. Maybe if I had been able to accept Rebecca's terminal prognosis myself, this might have been something she and I would have discussed. But I still don't think it would have been right to burden our kids with the horror of what was coming, and cloud their final weeks with their mum in misery and dread. It wasn't what Rebecca had wanted, and I trusted her judgement as a mother more than anything anyone else on this earth could say.

I was highly surprised, too, by how keen the experts seem to be on letting children see the body before it's buried. They think it helps make death real to kids. I think it sounds mad.

One thing I read did not surprise me at all. Women are *twice* as likely as men to get counselling. Magazines like to bang on about metrosexuals and New Men, but in reality most men would still rather go to the pub than to a therapist. I know the feeling very well myself.

But by now I was feeling a bit more confident about seeing what grief counsellors had to offer. Not long after meeting Nickey and Sarah I set off to Buckinghamshire, just north of London, to visit Child Bereavement UK, a nationwide charity which also runs family workshops. At its centres, children who have lost a parent get together and talk about what they're dealing with and how they're coping.

The branch near Milton Keynes is in a beautiful sort of country house, with nothing depressing or morbid about the set-up. The kids who were there that day came from all different types of background, and had experienced every kind of bereavement. They were a bit older than mine, the groups starting from eleven years old. Even so, I was blown away by the maturity I saw when they let me sit in on their meeting.

A girl called Rebecca had lost her mum twelve years earlier, when she was five, and was very clear about what a bereaved kid needs. 'You *have* to talk about the person. The person may not be here, but they're still a part of you, and that's not going to go away by pretending they don't exist, or they never existed.'

A young man called James made me think a lot about Lorenz. 'I didn't say anything to anyone for two years. I was just quiet. I didn't say a word. I just said I was fine.' He had been twelve when his dad died, and was nineteen now. 'But I found that coming here, I gained confidence, and felt I could speak honestly. Now I can speak to anyone about it.' A lot of the kids said they had found it easier to talk to other people, not their surviving parent, about how they were feeling, and I recognised that in my own kids, even though it was hard to hear.

One girl in particular caught my attention. Her name was Emily, and she was eighteen. Her mum had died of cancer when she was just eight, and she had been brought up by her dad, Mark. I hadn't been sure I'd want to do more than just observe the group, and didn't think I would want to get involved. But there was something about Emily that made me think of Tia, and after the meeting I asked if I could talk to Mark and Emily. I wanted to ask them some of the questions that were buzzing round my head. They agreed to let me visit them at home.

To look at Emily now, you would never have guessed what she had gone through in her short life. I was amazed when she said she had stopped going to school for two years when she was fourteen. She didn't look at all like your typical truant, and when she saw my surprise she grinned.

'I was a really good kid. But I just faked being sick for a long time.'

She had suffered from bad anxiety, she said, which is common for kids who have lost a parent, and that had put a strain on things with her dad. But the bond between them was so obviously powerful, I told myself that, if things got tough with my kids when they hit their teens, I'd remember to think about this girl.

If I could take only one of the experiences I had while making the documentary, it would probably be meeting Mark and Emily. If I was a train wreck of anxiety since Rebecca had died, Mark was the exact opposite. Even for a man who hadn't been through heartbreak, he would have struck anyone as unusually chilled out and relaxed. Maybe it was because he knew life had thrown its worst at him, and he had survived. In fact, he had done a lot more than just survive. He had brought up a daughter any father would be proud to call their own.

While Emily talked, all I kept thinking was, I hope Tia grows up to be like her. Was it possible? I hadn't believed it until now. But after all this girl had gone through, she was positive and strong, and I came away from Buckinghamshire with an unfamiliar sense of hope for my kids.

I came away with something else, too. I didn't know it as I drove home that day, but Mark and Emily had given me the key to a padlock I had begun to fear I would never unlock. For all these months I had felt as if I'd been trying different keys to unlock my kids' feelings, but none had fitted, and the padlock remained tightly shut. That was just about to change.

It's funny how solutions to the biggest problems in your life sometimes turn out to be the simplest little things. Emily had told me that after her mum died, her dad had given her a memory jar. Every time she remembered something about her mum, she would write the memory on a little piece of paper and pop it in the jar. She showed me the jar, and read out some of the memories she had written in it as a child.

'I remember when Mummy and Daddy took me to Watford to buy my witch's dress for Hallowe'en. And then we went trick or treating.' She smiled as she read it out, and said she wished she had written more down. Even something as simple as a trip with her mum to the supermarket would unlock more memories she now wished she could have.

The very next day I went out and bought a big, clear plastic jar shaped like a giant Coca-Cola bottle. I brought it home and explained to the kids how it worked.

'Here's a bit of paper for Lorenz. Here's a bit of paper for Tate. Here's a bit of paper for Tia.' I slid them across the dining-room table to where they sat, waiting and curious. 'And this,' I held up the jar, 'is where we put memories for Mummy. So whenever something comes into your mind – maybe that Mummy used to put funny videos on her phone—'

'Like the one of when she was jumping on the bed?' Tia interrupted.

'Exactly. And then any time you want, you come and take a piece of paper out and look, and it might give you a nice memory.'

What would they make of it? I wasn't sure. By then the

kids were used to having cameras in the house, as I had explained to them I was making a TV documentary, so they were unselfconscious about being filmed. I tried to look

confident as I explained the idea, but inside I was far from sure they would even give it a go. I wouldn't have been surprised if Lorenz had looked unimpressed and taken himself off to his room. What in fact happened next blew my mind.

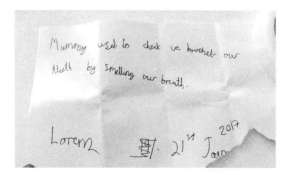

Suddenly, three kids who had refused to let me know what they were thinking were sitting round the kitchen table, tearing off strips of paper and scribbling down memories as fast as they could write.

Each time one thought of a new memory they would exclaim, 'Oh! Do you remember when Mum did this?' Or 'Oh! Oh! Oh! I've got one! I bet no one else remembers this!'

Lorenz wrote: 'Mummy used to check we brushed our teeth by smelling our breath', and 'Mummy used to watch *Casualty* with me every Saturday on her bed.'

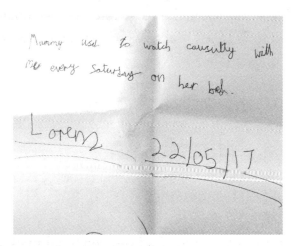

Tia wrote, 'I was in a trolley and I was crying because I wanted something to eat. Mummy gave me something before she paid.'

'I love doing this.' She smiled, busy drawing a picture of her mum. 'I'm going to start doing this every day.' I sat at the table and felt as if I was watching my family come back to life.

After that day, whenever anyone who had known Rebecca came to the house – which was practically everyone – one of the kids would lead them to the jar and insist they sit down at once and add a memory of their own. Tia's definition of a memory became increasingly elastic as she ran out of her own, so she began writing pretty much anything down, and into the jar it would go.

The mistake I've discovered people make with children who have lost their mum is to approach the subject with solemnity. That is literally the last thing kids want. They do not want people to talk about their mum in a voice that says, 'This is a *very sad* subject.' Once the memory jar was introduced, I soon saw that what they loved best were silly stories, funny stories, stories about their mum that would make everyone laugh. Best of all were ones about Rebecca and me, which cast me as the clown. Their favourite was the story about how she and I had met, and they would laugh every time I impersonated Rebecca telling me that, no, I would not be getting her phone number. They couldn't – and still can't – hear it enough times.

A few months later I had to go to Paris for work, to cover the Euro 2016 championship for the BBC. My mum and Sandra would look after the kids while I was away, but I was going to be away for Father's Day, so Mum organised a secret trip across the Channel. I have no idea how she managed to swear them all to secrecy – Tia is not exactly the soul of discretion – and they must have been beside themselves with excitement as they crept up behind me in the hotel lobby, to ambush me with squeals and hugs and kisses.

Mum had brought padlocks with her, engraved with Rebecca's name, mine and the children's. That afternoon we walked through Paris to what's known as Lovelock Bridge, across the Seine, on which thousands – maybe tens of thousands – of padlocks etched with loved ones' names have been secured to the railings by people from all over the world, just like us. The kids were glowing with excitement as we approached the bridge. It must have felt as if for once their mum was with them for a family outing again.

A curious kind of peace seemed to settle on us as we secured our padlocks to the bridge. But as I was getting to my feet, I happened to glance across at Lorenz. He was gazing out at the river, lost in thought. His expression was unreadable. I longed to ask what he was thinking, but knew it would be a waste of time. We might be making progress, but we still had a long way to go.

Lovelock Bridge, Paris

Here are some things I have learned. . .

- *Kids can recover from losing a parent – but only with the right help*
The bad news is that children who lose a parent are at risk of all sorts of long-term problems. In one study, teachers reported that children who'd lost a parent were significantly more withdrawn, anxious, depressed, aggressive and delinquent. Other studies have found them more prone to depression, anxiety and addiction in adulthood – and bereaved boys seem to be more vulnerable than girls.

But the good news is that there's a lot we can do to help them grow up without facing these problems. Sheryl Sandberg, the chief operating officer of Facebook, lost her husband very suddenly in 2015, and has written about how it's possible to achieve 'post-traumatic growth' for herself and her children. She believes children can suffer a major trauma like the death of a parent but emerge stronger and more resilient, as long as they get the support they need.

Julia Samuel is the grief psychotherapist who is also Founder Patron of Child Bereavement UK, and her book, *Grief Works*, offers some practical things you can do to support bereaved children.

- *Tell them the truth*
It sounds deceptively simple, but telling them the truth is

massively important. 'Children need to be given as much information as adults,' Samuel says, 'and it should be conveyed in age-appropriate and concrete language. What they don't know, they tend to make up, and what they make up can be much worse than the truth.'

- *Involve them in the funeral*
It's also incredibly important to let children go to the funeral. Explain the point of a funeral and tell them what is likely to happen, so they won't be overwhelmed on the day.

- *Stick to normal routines*
Try to keep their regular routines going, even when you feel as if your whole world has turned upside down. Familiar boundaries and structures help make kids feel safe and secure. The uncertainty and upset in routine that comes with a parent dying can be bewildering, so it's best to stick to regular routines and normal discipline as much as possible.

- *Talk, talk, talk*
Above all, you can never talk too much about the parent they have lost. All kids, but particularly those so young they can barely remember the parent they've lost, need to hear stories and memories to help them build up a clear picture of the person who died. For my kids, the memory jar has been invaluable, and I can't recommend it enough.

- *Keep it simple*
Bereaved kids don't need grand gestures or extravagant treats. What they really want, more than anything, is your time

and attention. If at all possible, try to find opportunities to spend some one-on-one time with them, without their siblings. You don't need to fly them to the moon: a weekly trip to Nando's will do just as well.

• *There are some incredible organisations out there, so use them*
If you're anything like me, you might find it hard to ask for help. You may feel too proud, or afraid – or maybe you don't believe anyone could possibly understand what your kids are going through or know what they need. But trust me, there's no shame in asking for help. You'll be amazed at what's out there.

Some of the charities you could try are listed in Where to Find Help (pages 259–61).

CHAPTER THIRTEEN

Not Alone

IT IS 28 March 2017. I'm at home, in the kitchen. The kids are upstairs asleep, and Sandra is in her bedroom. I turn on the television, and switch over to BBC1. It is nine o'clock.

'I had an unbelievable life,' I hear my voice saying. 'An amazing wife, great kids. Then: bang. It all changed.'

I've been watching myself on TV for twenty years. I'm used to it. Nowadays I'm even a TV studio pundit: being on telly is my job. But I have never stood in my kitchen and watched it on the screen. The sensation is weirdly disorienting. But stranger than that – much, much stranger – is the sight of me on television breaking down in tears. I've cried in public before, but only ever on the football field and at funerals. Over the course of the next hour I'm going to be choking with guttural tears in front of the whole country.

By 9.03 p.m. my phone is going berserk. My phone is always fairly busy – I like WhatsApp groups and silly joke texts, so I'm used to seeing it buzz probably more than most. But this is unlike anything I've ever seen. Every message I try to read is interrupted by a new torrent of incoming traffic. And the strangest thing of all? Every single one is basically saying the same thing: 'This film is incredible, well done and thank you.'

When you play professional football, you grow accustomed to provoking a big public response. But football is a competitive sport, and opinion is therefore by definition always divided. Over the years I've had to grow a very thick skin, because for every fan there is someone out there who hates you and what you do with an equally visceral passion. There's no such thing as a global critical consensus about a footballer. Even Lionel Messi, probably the world's most loved player, has his haters.

My phone carries on going nuts, but not one negative comment appears on the screen. Not one. I cannot believe my eyes. I don't know what I was expecting but it wasn't this.

THIS MAY SOUND a bit implausible, or disingenuous, but throughout the making of the documentary all I thought about was the impact it would have on myself and my children. They were used to seeing me cry. Seeing themselves and their lives on the screen, though, and watching me try to open up and ask for help for us all, would be completely new to them. Sometimes I used to try to imagine them being older, and mature enough to watch it, and wondered how they would feel. But the viewing public? I barely gave them a thought.

That changed a month or so before the documentary was

due to be broadcast, when I had a meeting with a woman at the BBC in charge of scheduling. I have a terrible habit of losing concentration during meetings, and my mind was beginning to wander off when I vaguely heard what she was saying. Suddenly I snapped back into focus.

'So we're thinking nine p.m. on BBC1. Everyone's agreed.'

Did I hear that right? I asked her to repeat it.

FUCKING HELL. BBC1. Nine p.m., primetime? That was the moment when it began to dawn on me that the film we had made would be watched not just by me, my friends, family, and one day my kids. A lollipop lady in Norfolk, a sheep farmer in Scotland, the girl behind the counter in our local Costa Coffee might all watch it too. I was stunned.

I think the second most stressful day of my life after the day Rebecca died came about a week later when we held two private screenings of the film before it went out on the BBC. A cinema room in the basement of a hotel on the South Bank was booked, and the first showing was to be mainly for journalists and critics. Ben Brooks-Dutton was there, with the other widowers I had met that day with him, and Gary Lineker was also in the audience. Everyone gathered in a reception area next to the screening room for drinks and biscuits before it began, but I arrived in such a jangle of nerves that it took me a good hour to settle down enough even to register their presence.

'Rio. What's wrong with you? Just calm down.' My PA took one look at me, and I saw the concern in her expression.

'What do you mean? What are you talking about?' It's a

measure of my extreme anxiety that I'd lost all self-awareness, and couldn't even understand what she meant.

'Rio, it's like a tornado just walked in. You're going at a million miles a minute. Listen, there's a little room over there. It's been reserved for you and close family. Just chill in there for a bit. Go and have a drink or something. Just calm down.'

I don't think I'd ever suffered from performance anxiety before in my life. I'm used to playing in huge football matches, watched by millions all over the world. I don't do nerves. Ice-cold steel was a big part of my identity as a player. But as I sat in that little room while the film was screened, I could actually hear my own heart racing. What would everyone say when they had seen the film? I just hoped and prayed they would feel I had done justice to Rebecca and her memory.

We had arranged for a little Q and A on stage afterwards, with myself and the BBC producer of the film. The lights had already come up when I walked in. As I scanned the rows, all I could see was people in tears. Hands were clutching tissues; grown men were sniffling. Gary Lineker had nearly lost his son to cancer when he was just a baby. Normally he and I would do that typical blokey kind of greeting, but when I saw his red eyes it hit me that nothing about today was going to be normal. As I settled into a chair on the stage, it was all I could do to stop myself breaking down.

In so far as I had thought about the critical response to the film, my main worry had been that people might think I was somehow glorifying myself. In my mind, to allow TV cameras into your home had always been a signifier of someone obsessed with maximising their fame. Would people think I was exploiting my family and invading my own privacy to raise my profile? Enhance my brand? That the film would instead make people cry hadn't even occurred to me.

When the Q and A was over, that was only the first hurdle out of the way. The much more daunting one was coming next. The second screening, which was about to start, was for family and friends of Rebecca and me. This audience wasn't here because of me: they were here because of her. I was half out of my mind with worry. What would they think? What would they make of it? I sat next to my mum to watch, and as the lights dimmed every muscle in my body tensed.

When the lights came up at the end, I looked around and once again saw rows of streaming faces. In one sense it was less surprising this time because all these people had known and loved Rebecca. But what hadn't occurred to me until now was that the film might make them draw parallels with other losses they had suffered in their lives as well.

One of my oldest and closest friends approached me, choked up with tears. When he was a teenager his brother had been shot in the chest, over a stupid little row about something, and died. I have known him since we were seven or eight and, by the standards of my circles, would have said he was one of the more emotionally open men I knew. He took my arm. 'Listen, man, that really got me thinking about my brother. All this whole time, you know, I haven't grieved. He was killed twenty-two years ago, and you know what that film just did? It made me realise I still haven't ever really grieved for him.'

When the day of the BBC1 broadcast came, I felt drained. I'd done quite a lot of publicity in the preceding fortnight, giving press, radio and TV interviews. I was talked out. Making the documentary had taken more of a toll than I think I'd realised at the time, and it was only much later, when people close to me, like Jamie, said they had watched me sink lower and lower while I relived the nightmare of Rebecca's death, that I appreciated quite what the film had cost me. By doing the publicity, I'd had to relive it all over again. I felt shattered.

That evening my phone began to catch fire from about six o'clock. The kids were still up, clattering around the house, and maybe because half my mind was on them, and not the messages beginning to flood in, I read the first with an element of scepticism. Emotional exhaustion was making me even more wary than normal. But most of the messages were from strangers on social media, and it's just a fact that some people will say anything online to make them feel connected to a famous footballer. When I was a boy, as you may remember, my dad taught me to distrust praise from youth football coaches – because what did they care whether I had genuinely played well or not? So when random strangers began messaging me to say the film was going to be 'a-*maaaaaazing*', I took it with a pinch of salt.

By 9.03 p.m. it was friends and family messaging me to say they were watching and already weeping, and I started to take the consensus much more seriously. What took me completely by surprise were the texts that quickly followed from people at the BBC. From senior executives to the young runners on the crew, everyone was telling me how proud they felt to have been involved in the project.

More than six and a half million people watched the documentary that night. Since then even more millions have watched it online – and that was just in the UK. Letters and emails poured into the BBC, and are still arriving now.

The letters reinforced for me just how common it is for people, especially men, to try to dodge grief by blocking out their emotions. Drinking or working too much are, as you'll see, classic avoidance techniques. The letters showed me, once again, the importance of opening up a conversation. The first step is always the hardest, and most of us need help to take it. I was touched by them and have included a few in 'Letters of Support' (see pages 253–8).

As a footballer, you're used to making a big impact on people. The game inspires passions; that's one of the things I've always loved most about it. Ultimately, however, you can make or break someone's Saturday afternoon – but you do not actually affect people at the deepest level of their private lives. I began to see that what we had made with the BBC went way beyond anything I had ever achieved on the field. I could have won ten Premier League titles, and that still would not compete with the impact of this. We weren't just touching people, we were actually helping them.

Everywhere I go now, people come up to tell me about what the film meant to them. The demographic of strangers who approach me in the street has changed beyond all recognition. The walk from our office in town to the nearest branch of Pret a Manger can't be more than a hundred yards, but in the time it takes me to pop out and grab a sandwich I can be approached by little old ladies, City businessmen, Japanese waiters. Sometimes a butch bald bloke will approach me while my kids are playing football, and automatically I still assume he will be a Man United fan. Instead he wants to tell me about the death of his mother, and breaks down in tears on my shoulder.

I wasn't prepared for this. I take it as confirmation that we were right to make the film, because it has clearly tapped into a need deeper than anything any of us could have dreamed of. Men don't have role models to show them how to mourn, so most of us have no idea how to, or even how to ask for help. I also, however, found the public response excruciatingly uncomfortable. I don't think I need to spell out by now just how awkward I am with accelerated intimacy, and unfamiliar with this kind of thing. It is still all new to me, and I have no techniques for handling it. Strangers tell me the most gut-wrenching, heartrending tales of tragedy and loss, and I don't know what to say.

'Thanks'?

'That's a shame'?

These responses aren't just inadequate but ridiculous. But what would be the right thing to say?

I find praise almost as difficult to receive. When people tell me, 'What you did in that documentary was incredible. It was such a good thing', I still don't know how to respond. If I had my way, Rebecca would still be here, so these people are praising a piece of work I wish had no reason to exist. I reassure myself that out of this catastrophe we have managed to salvage something positive – and we have. But what I should probably do is come up with some suitable handy phrases to learn off by heart so I don't keep finding myself stuck for anything sensible to say.

At the beginning of this journey I knew I needed help to come to terms with a death. I knew I needed help to learn to grieve. Along the way, what I have discovered is that practically everyone else does too.

We seem to have created a world where death is considered abnormal, as if it were some kind of freak aberration. We go about our lives pretending it won't happen to anyone we love – and when it does, we can't believe it. It's bizarre when you stop and think about it. We go through life constantly preparing for the next stage – at school we revise for exams; then when we leave, we rehearse for job interviews, and on it goes. We wouldn't dream of blundering into an important challenge blind – and no one knows this better than professional sportspeople. David Beckham did not get to take the best free kicks in the world because the fairies sprinkled magic on his boots. He got to be the best in the world by practising and preparing, over and over and over again.

I said at the very start of this book that I wasn't going to pretend I'm now some sort of grief expert. I'm not, and I won't. But I do wonder why schools don't teach children about death, as a standard part of the curriculum. We're taught about birth at school, yet the one thing we know about every creature ever born is that one day it will die. And we do nothing to prepare ourselves for it. When it happens, we don't know what to do.

Here are some things I have learned

- *Men often look for help in the wrong places*

Alcohol

When I began to drink heavily after Rebecca went into hospital, I had no idea how common it was for men to look for comfort in a bottle. One study has found that the bereaved made up a quarter of admissions to alcohol rehab centres. One in five widowers, according to another study, drink to dangerous levels.

At the time, it feels like it will help. In actual fact, alcohol messes up your sleep, your appetite, your concentration. In other words, it only makes the problems you're probably already facing even worse. Take it from me, it is not a good idea.

Work

Workaholism is another very common response to grief in men. Frenetic activity drains your energy and leaves you physically exhausted and emotionally numb   which, when you're in despair, can seem very appealing. Most workaholics have suffered some kind of major trauma, and it's their way of coping – only, once again, it's nothing like as effective as we think. Keeping busy is a short-term strategy but not a long-term solution. It just delays the recovery process by keeping you from facing your feelings.

Suicide

Thoughts of suicide are also unbelievably common among the bereaved. One study found that 65 per cent of widowers had thoughts of wanting to die. Of that group, one in ten had made an actual suicide attempt, and more than a third had engaged in self-destructive behaviour – drinking, drug-taking or other self-harm. I don't think I need to spell out why suicide is not a solution. But if you are having these sorts of thoughts, remind yourself that they are quite normal, and nothing to be angry with yourself about. Talk to your GP, or ask for help from one of the organisations listed in Where to Find Help (pages 259–61).

I know that none of these coping strategies work – because I tried or thought about them all. What did help me, though, was physical training. The endorphins released by exercise help literally everything – your mood, your stress, your sleep and your energy levels. It's hard to get to the gym when you're miserable – especially if you're drinking or working insane hours. If you can afford it, a personal trainer really helps. If not – and most people can't – get a friend to train with you. It will make all the difference. A training partner will still get you into the gym on those days when you don't even want to get out of bed. Grief also plays havoc with your appetite, but I've found that training helps regulate it, and encourages me to eat well.

CHAPTER FOURTEEN

Finding Our Way

IT'S JUNE 2017. It's a warm summer's evening, and Tate and Tia are already asleep in their beds. It is Lorenz's bedtime now, but as he gets to his feet to climb the stairs he turns and looks at me. 'Dad. Would you come and lie with me for a bit?'

'Sure, Lorenz. Of course.' I follow him into his bedroom and we lie down side by side, gazing up at the ceiling. From the corner of my eye, in the summer's evening light, I can see that he's smiling.

We do this quite a lot now. He doesn't like to come into my bed for cuddles. He isn't tactile enough for that. But more and more, these days, he asks me to come and lie with him at bedtime – just like his mum used to do. Without shifting his gaze from the ceiling, Lorenz nudges me. 'This is nice, isn't it, Dad? This is nice.'

REBECCA'S DEATH CHANGED our lives for ever. As I write this now, a little more than two years later, I can see that it has also changed me as a man, and as a father. I just spent the

223

weekend alone with Lorenz, while Tate and Tia were with their grandparents, and I know this will sound like a tiny thing to most people, but to me it was massive. We'd had a perfect weekend together, doing little low-key things – going out to eat, seeing a movie, playing football. His brother and sister would soon be arriving home, and we were reaching that point on a Sunday when you need to start thinking about baths and hair-washing and school bags for the morning. My work diary for Monday was looking hectic – there were a million and one things to get ready.

But as we got home and stood in the hallway, taking off our shoes, I paused, and turned to Lorenz, and ruffled his hair. 'How good was that? We had a wicked weekend, didn't we?'

He looked up and smiled. 'Yeah, Dad, we did.'

I cannot remember my dad ever showing pleasure in my company when I was a boy, let alone telling me he did. I know he felt it – but to say something like that would have been unimaginable to him. It would have meant the world to me, though. Showing Lorenz love in such a simple way, by telling him, still did not come naturally to me, and I had to consciously remind myself to do it. But looking into Lorenz's smiling eyes, I saw what it meant for him.

The children have all seen a counsellor at school since their mum died. A number of other kids at their school have been bereaved, so there was already a full-time counsellor on the staff when Rebecca died. My three see her once a week. She and I spoke recently, and she told me she can see a big improvement in their willingness to talk about Rebecca, and how they miss her. It wasn't always like that, she said.

Tia is back in her own bed now. She is still allowed to sleep in mine at the weekends, and Tate pads in most mornings, bleary-eyed, and clambers in for a cuddle. But whatever loneliness the night held for them is now, I hope, beginning to fade. They wear Rebecca's old cardigans or pyjama tops in bed, and God help whoever moves them while they're tidying up. The clothes live under the kids' pillows, and are not going anywhere.

I wonder all the time about their future, and who my kids will become as they get older. Already I can see that Tia's memories of her mum are fading, and even for the boys each passing year will make their memories of Rebecca less intensely immediate, and more abstract. I try to comfort myself with something grief experts often say. Bereaved children may forget the parent they have lost, but they never forget the love that parent showed them when they were alive. In my more panicky moments I worry about how they will navigate all the dramas of their teenage years without a mother, and I worry most for Tia as she gets older and needs a woman in her life. But I don't think anyone who meets the children today would guess what they have been through. They are strikingly confident kids, unfazed by anything. Tate will talk to anyone, Lorenz has just played the lead role in his school play and Tia is always herself in any situation.

I have tried to put systems in place so that I can spend more time with the kids. My team know that my diary should let me be home for supper on Mondays and Fridays, and we do our best to limit my trips away to midweek. It isn't always possible, but we try. I try, too, to make sure the children get time alone with me. On Wednesdays now I take Tia to Nando's, and she loves fetching the cutlery, and setting up the table and chatting to the waitresses. Even just ten minutes alone in the car with me is worth more to my kids than I ever used to understand. It's funny, when I think about it, because that is what I always wanted with my dad. But I used to be too afraid of him to ask.

Rebecca knew and understood all of this. She didn't need anyone to tell her to go upstairs and lie with one of the kids for fifteen minutes for no other reason than that it made them happy. When the kids had been toddlers she used to love to bake with them, or paint with them, or bundle them into the car with a picnic and take them off to a park for the day. On rainy afternoons she would snuggle them all up with her on the sofa, close the curtains, dim the lights, put on a DVD and pretend they were at the movies, with giant bowls of popcorn and ice cream. She could spend hours on the trampoline with the kids, goofing about, and on holiday would happily splash around, playing with them in the pool from dawn till dusk.

Birthday parties were always themed extravaganzas. For the boys' birthdays, she would tell guests to come in football kit, fill the garden with goal posts and organise penalty shoot-out games. Hallowe'en was her favourite excuse for a big party, and everyone had to come in costume. She never minded making herself look ridiculous. One year she dressed up as a pumpkin; another time she was Dracula. When we moved back to London from Manchester she threw a leaving party for all the kids' school friends and hired a fun fair to turn the garden into a mini Alton Towers for the day.

I've had to be taught this stuff – but I'm learning. Slowly but surely, I'm learning. The heartbreaking truth is that losing Rebecca has made me more loving. I can't turn back the clock and show her more love, but I can try not to repeat the same mistakes with our children. My guilt about the past is something I will always have to live with. I couldn't live with myself if I denied my kids the affection they need now, too.

When I used to see people weep at a movie, I always felt scornful and confused. What was wrong with them? Nowadays I can cry at the drop of a hat, and I see that the person who had something wrong with them for all those years wasn't them, it was me. Funnily enough, the other day my dad said something similar. He never used to cry either. Now when he watches programmes about slavery, he finds his eyes welling up. Being able to cry makes me feel more alive, and for that I am profoundly grateful.

I no longer have days when all I can do is cancel my plans and curl up in a ball. It is only nights that can still undo me. I usually wake up between two and three a.m., when the horror of what my children have lost hits me again, keeping me awake until dawn. I have learned that we can survive without Rebecca, but in those lonely dark hours I am still winded by sadness for my kids.

Sometimes people tell me I should count my blessings, because I still have three beautiful, healthy children. To be honest, it winds me up a bit when they say that. I lost the love of my life, my children lost their mother – and they want me to be whoopee-doo-isn't-life-great? But some evenings I do look around the table and think, There are still four of us here. If that's counting my blessings, then I guess I do.

Lorenz still worries me, mostly because his silences remind me so much of myself. Tate and Tia continue to fill the memory jar, but Lorenz has gradually withdrawn from it and will seldom get involved now. He has a way of retreating into himself that makes me feel as if I'm looking in the mirror. I'm still trying to work out how to help him open up.

Of course, in many ways I haven't changed either. I am still unbelievably disorganised. I'm messy, and chaotic, and forgetful. I have to force myself to be more open and affectionate, and to talk more about how I'm feeling. If you met me for the first time today, you'd probably think I was a bit of a closed book, and might say I was a cold fish. All I can tell you is, trust me, you wouldn't if you'd known what I was like for the first thirty-six years of my life. Family culture is a very powerful thing, and you don't get to change it like a lightbulb.

Family dynamics are complicated, too. Remove Rebecca from the picture of our wider families, and all the other bits of the jigsaw are still there, but sometimes it feels as if the pieces have been tossed into the air and fallen all over the place. A death affects everyone differently, and all of us have suffered our own trauma. When emotions are all over the place, and hearts are breaking, it can be hard to stay mindful of others' feelings, and easy to hurt them inadvertently. One of the biggest things I've learned about bereavement is how much patience and understanding are required.

We're all struggling to put ourselves back together and work out how to be a family now that Rebecca is no longer with us. She was always the glue, the diplomat, the buffer. Without her I don't think we've quite worked out how to make a new jigsaw that fits for everyone.

WHILE REBECCA LAY dying in the Royal Marsden, her best friend, Lisa, visited almost every day. Lisa is the wife of Jamie, my agent, and she and Rebecca were as close as friends can be. Rebecca told Lisa something in the final weeks of her life, and months later Lisa told me what it was.

'It kills me to think of Rio with a new partner, Lisa. You know it does. Of course it does. But you know what kills me even more? Thinking of him alone and lonely. If I don't make it, Lisa, I don't want Rio to be miserable. I want him to be happy.'

With Mum and Anton

I know the kids think about me dating again. My brother, Anton, got married in Italy last summer, and when it was announced at the wedding that the first dance would take place in twenty minutes, Tate came and sat on my lap. Ordinarily he would be off again in a second, flying about, but twenty minutes later he was still in my lap. After the first dance finished, he got up. 'I'm going to bed now, Dad. But listen to me. You're not going to dance with no one, are you?'

'What do you mean, Tate?'

'If you dance, dance with Nanny,' meaning my mum, 'or with Chloe,' my sister. 'That's it. Don't dance with no one else.'

I sat there and thought: Wow. So *that*'s what's on his mind.

Just the other day I was driving the kids to school and we got talking about the prom coming up for Lorenz at the end of term. 'You taking a girl from class?' I asked.

'I might,' he said. 'I don't know yet. I've got a couple of options.'

'Yeah?' I grinned. 'Okay. So what about if I was going to a prom? Who would I take?'

Tate's features darkened. 'You're not going on a date with no one. You don't need to go on a date with no one, Dad.'

Tia chimed in: 'Well, we don't want him to be lonely, do we? We don't want Dad to be lonely. So, Dad, you can go with me.'

'Yes, but can't I go with any of my friends?'

'Well who?' Tia asked. I ran through a few names, just family friends, to see how they would react.

'No chance.' Tate shook his head firmly. 'No.'

When I picked them up from school that afternoon, the first thing Tate said as he ran up to me was 'Dad, you're not going on a date, are you?' He plonked himself firmly in my lap.

Tia's class appeared next, and she ran over and joined us. 'Have you found a date yet, Dad? You found a date?'

If I try to picture a future alone, the bleak unending loneliness of it can sometimes almost suffocate me. But when I try to picture introducing a new partner into our lives, my mind reels until I'm dizzy. I look around at the home Rebecca built for us, and think, No way could we ever leave this. I could never take my children away from this house. But, then, I also know that staying in the past is not going to be helpful for any new relationship I may have.

I guess we'll cross that bridge if and when we get to it.

Right now I have something much more momentous and urgent on my mind. I hadn't thought my heart could break into any more pieces. I hadn't thought I could ever hurt as much again. I didn't think Fate could be any crueller. I didn't think life could get any worse.

But it has.

CHAPTER FIFTEEN

Mum

IT'S BREAKFAST TIME. We're at home, getting ready for the school day. The kids are at the table, wolfing down toast and cereal, while I rush around wiping surfaces and clearing away plates. We're not late – not yet, anyway – but I've got one eye on the clock.

Tia is doodling in her scrapbook while she eats, and Tate and Lorenz are arguing about which of them can run the fastest. It is a perennial dispute, and will never be resolved, no matter how many times they race, because invariably the loser comes up with some reason why that particular result shouldn't count.

'But you got a head start!' Tate is protesting to Lorenz.

'No, I didn't!' Lorenz maintains coolly. 'You were just slow off the mark.'

'Dad!' Tate appeals to me. 'This isn't fair! Tell him, Dad.'

I look across the kitchen at my three children. I can still remember when a contest with my brother had felt to me like the most important thing in the world – and right now I would give anything to go back to being that boy again.

233

It's a weird feeling to be jealous of one's own children, but at this moment I envy their innocence. I envy them for what they do not know.

The kids have no idea that, after they leave for school, I will drive into London to sit at the hospital bedside of the woman they love who is dying of cancer. Machines will beep and flash pitilessly, as if counting down the final seconds, hours, days of her life. Already, she is losing the power of speech.

I know that I will have to tell the children soon. I can't keep putting it off. But when I try to picture myself finding the words, I begin to feel faint. How can I break their hearts like that? And so I will keep putting it off for another day. This evening I won't mention where I've been.

'Come on, kids,' I call brightly. 'Time to get in the car. Time for school. Sandra's dropping you this morning.'

As they grab their bags and kiss me goodbye, I am disoriented by déjà vu. Because this is not April 2015. It is June 2017. This time it isn't their mum who lies dying of cancer. It is mine.

SHORTLY BEFORE CHRISTMAS in 2015, seven months after Rebecca died, my mum had gone to her doctor, concerned about her bladder, and received chilling news.

'We need to run a lot of tests. It could be nothing. But I have to be honest with you, it could be cancer.'

Mum didn't tell a soul. For the first few weeks she didn't even tell Peter, her husband. She struggled on, managing the pain and discomfort privately, and just before Christmas her doctor confirmed her worst fears. She had cancer.

Even then, the only person she told was Peter. It was going to be our first Christmas without Rebecca, and Mum didn't want to make it any harder than it would already be. We spent Christmas Day together, and on Boxing Day the kids and I flew off to Cape Verde to see in the new year, oblivious to the new medical catastrophe unfolding within the family.

Mum sent a message when we got back, asking me to come to hers for supper. I didn't know that she had also sent Anton a message, asking him to come on a spurious pretext to collect something. When I arrived our sister Sian was there, too, equally in the dark. I was busy telling her about our trip to Cape Verde when Mum asked us all to sit down. Something in her expression caught us all, and silenced the room. Mum has never been a particularly formal person, and when she announced, 'I'm afraid I've got something to tell you all,' I turned cold.

'I've got cancer,' she said. 'It's in my bladder. On Wednesday I'm going to have an operation. They're going to carry out a full hysterectomy, and they're going to remove my bladder and replace it with a new one.'

I couldn't believe what I was hearing. None of us could. We broke down, inconsolably distraught, and I was still shaking when my mum drove me to my dad's and dropped me there. I was thirty-eight years old, but felt like an eight-year-old boy. I needed my parents, and could barely comprehend what was happening.

When the Wednesday came I went to hospital with Mum. She was in surgery for nine hours, then transferred straight to intensive care, where I sat with her through the night. Never have I been so glad to see the dawn. It had been one of the most frightening nights of my life. From a hospital window I watched the sun rise, and prayed to a God I don't even believe in to make my mum okay.

For a while it looked as if the prayers had been answered. Within six weeks she seemed back to her old self. Mum cannot stand sympathy so she'd kept the operation secret, and told nobody beyond close family. She didn't even want my kids to know, and neither did I. They had already suffered too much.

And for well over a year, it looked as if she was going to make a full recovery. I thought they would never need to know. When I began writing this book, in the spring of the following year, Mum seemed as fit and well as she had ever been. She was in and out of our house every day, collecting the kids from school or ferrying them about to horse-riding and playdates. She wore a Fitbit, and liked to walk from ours to Jamie and Lisa's. Her daily target was ten thousand steps, and most days she was hitting it.

Then came the bombshell. Mum and Peter came over to ours for a meal. They invited Anton too, but I noticed nothing strained in the atmosphere, until the kids were upstairs in bed and suddenly Mum's expression changed.

'I've got something to tell you,' she announced. The table froze. I looked at my mum, and in that instant knew exactly what she was about to say.

'It's come back. The cancer. It's come back.'

That was early June – a month ago. Mum was admitted to hospital a few days later, and has been there ever since. The parallels with Rebecca are eerie: the cancer has spread to Mum's bones and liver, as well as her kidney and lung.

The doctors have tried chemotherapy, but it didn't work. They've tried other drugs, but again with no success. As I write these words, we're waiting for Mum to start a new course of treatment, and there are days when she seems to rally – but there are others when her condition nose-dives and she cannot move or speak. Everything feels hauntingly familiar. And yet this time round, everything is very different.

I'm not proud to have to admit that for the first few days I could not bring myself to visit Mum in hospital. She isn't in the Royal Marsden, thank God, but the thought of sitting on another oncology ward, next to those same awful machines, hearing the same beeps, breathing in that same antiseptic smell, was more than I could face. I never wanted to see any of it ever again.

When I forced myself into the car and drove to the hospital near London Bridge, I thought I'd got a grip on myself. I thought I could deal with it. I pulled up in the car park, took a deep breath, reached out to the door handle – and let my hand fall. As if in a trance, I felt all my strength ebb away, leaving me slumped and dazed at the wheel. I couldn't open the door. I couldn't get out of the car.

I don't know how long I sat there before Mum began phoning.

'Where are you, Rio? I thought you'd be here by now. What's holding you up?'

How could I tell her I was already there? 'Sorry, Mum, I'm running late. I'm on my way. I'll be there really soon,' I promised, hating myself for my weakness. But still I couldn't rouse myself from that weird paralysis. I sat there in the car park for two hours.

Come on, Rio, I tried to tell myself. Pull yourself together. You've always known your parents weren't going to live for ever. No one's do. You're thirty-eight years old, man. This is the natural order of things. Deal with it.

But what use was logic when I was beyond reason and deaf to sense? In my head all I could hear were my frantic pleas for divine reprieve. *Please, no, not my mum.* Anyone but my mum. She was the only reason why I survived losing Rebecca. Please, don't take her too. There are seven billion

other people on this planet, and not one of them can ever know or love me the way she always has. What she means to me is more than I can lose.

A talent for football might look like the great blessing of my life, but without her love and support what good would it have been to me? The real luck of my life was my mum. Yes, I was fortunate to be born with a gift for kicking a ball – but plenty of other boys are, too, and very few ever make it to the top. Talent alone would not have lifted me out of Peckham. Without my mum by my side every step of the way I could never have made it. Everything I have achieved in my life, and everything I have today, I owe to her. And now she's dying. It's more than I can bear.

As a footballer I was trained to assess even the most inauspicious situation as winnable, so under normal circumstances positive thinking is second nature to me. But finding a silver lining in the death of my mum, within three years of my wife's, is a very tall order. All I can come up with is one bittersweet consolation. After all my regret for learning to love and grieve too late to help Rebecca, I guess I have now been given a second chance. I'm not going to make the same mistakes again.

My old coping mechanism was denial, but not this time. Instead, I see it in my siblings. The optimism of youth has strapped Jeremiah, still just eighteen, Sian, only twenty-three and even Anton, at thirty-two, onto a rollercoaster of hope and disappointment. I recognise it all too well, for it's the same white-knuckle ride I clung to in the Royal Marsden, addicted to the fleeting euphoria of those days when the drugs seemed to be working, and blind to the overwhelming evidence that they weren't. I watch them seize on the flim-siest suggestion of improvement, and draw wildly unrealistic conclusions from any random visitor's hopeful opinion that they can see 'definite progress'.

I understand the opiate allure of denial. Of course I do. But I've been here before, and can't be fooled twice. When I look into my mum's eyes, I recognise what I see. I know she's dying, and so does she.

On days when speech is beyond her, I hold her hand in mine and we gaze at one another in silence. Sometimes I lean in and whisper in her ear, telling her how much I love her and what she means to me. But if she can talk, I don't want to waste the time. I ask about her wishes for her funeral, for family arrangements in the future, for practicalities following her death. I write it all down. I need to know what she wants, and how I can help Peter. He has been the best husband I could ever have wanted for her, and is now facing the enormity of single parenthood, which I know all too well.

What's frustrating me is how hard I still find it to show my siblings affection and compassion, even now. In my head I'm fighting a constant battle with my inhibitions, but no matter how sternly I tell myself to give them a big hug and ask how they're feeling, my old cold awkwardness keeps winning. Jeremiah is still a hormonal teenager, and I worry desperately about how he and Sian will cope. For now, though, all I can offer them is the wisdom of my experience, and hope they can hear it.

'Listen,' I tell them. 'I've been through this situation before. I went through it with Rebecca. Don't make the mistakes I made. Use this time to tell Mum how much you love her. Tell her every day. Anything you want to say or ask, do it now. Dot all the *is*, cross all the *ts*, say goodbye properly. Trust me, if you don't you're going to regret it. You do not want be haunted every night by the things you left unsaid. Say them now.'

Something else has changed in me, too. If I could have it my way, Mum would live for ever – but the reality is, she's dying. She's in constant unimaginable pain, diminished and traumatised by each new course of treatment. She's had enough. For her whole life, my mum has always been the pack leader, taking care of everyone else, putting our needs first. It's the only way she knows how to be. Now cancer has made her a stranger to herself, reducing her to a helpless patient who can barely recognise herself.

'I'm so sorry,' she keeps apologising. 'I'm so sorry for letting you all down. I'm so sorry for letting your kids down, Rio. They need me so badly, and I should be there for them. I was meant to be there for them while they grew up. I'm so sorry.'

'Mum,' I try to reassure her, 'please, this is madness. You have nothing to apologise for. You must know that. You've devoted your whole life to us, Mum, and given us everything. Please, please, stop this mad chat about saying sorry There's no need for sorrys here. The only words that need saying are thank you – by us to you. We'll be thanking you in our hearts every day for the rest of our lives,' I grin, trying to make her smile, 'and you'd better bloody well get that into your head, all right?'

But while I won't go along with any of her mad 'sorry'

nonsense, there is something else she wants to say, which I do not try to silence. I do not tell her she's chatting rubbish. I do not argue her out of it. Every impulse in me wants to stand up and scream, 'No! No, no, no, I am not going to let that happen.' But I don't.

By now her voice has shrivelled to a feeble, husky whisper. She knows she can't have many words left, and every croak costs her too much effort and pain to waste on anything unimportant. I know she's being deadly serious when she gazes into the eyes of her children and Peter, gathered around her bed, and tells us: 'I've had enough. Everything hurts. It hurts too much. If the next drug they try doesn't work either, I want the doctors to stop. I want them to let me go.'

I used to think nothing could matter more than life. But having now witnessed both birth and death, I think how a life ends matters just as much as how it begins. When someone we love is dying we feel helpless. But if we can honour their final wish, and give them the death they want, perhaps that is the ultimate act of love.

Our mum has devoted her entire life to her family. I don't think she should have to stay alive in terrible pain just because her children cannot bear to let her go. If the first selfish choice she ever makes will be her last, so be it. She has earned the right to put herself first, and I will always respect her decision.

'KIDS, I'VE GOT a bit of bad news to tell you. Nan's in hospital.' I glanced in the rear-view mirror and studied their faces to see how this had been received. I'd been fretting for days about how to announce it. They needed to get the message that the situation was serious, but I didn't want to make them panic and freak out.

'Why?' Tate demanded. 'What's wrong with her?'

A few days earlier I had consulted the school counsellor, who had been supporting the kids since Rebecca died. Her advice was to be as honest and open as I could be, but I still wasn't quite ready to break the news to them that it was cancer again.

'Oh, the doctors think she's got a virus. They're doing lots of tests to work out what it is, so that they can try and make her better.'

'So it's a bug, then?' asked Lorenz.

'Silly Nanny!' Tia giggled. 'She's gone and swallowed a bug!'

This half-truth bought me a bit more time, but the full story would become horribly clear as soon as the kids saw Mum in hospital. A few days later we were on our way to visit her when I turned the car stereo down and forced out the words I had been dreading.

'Listen, I've got something to tell you. They've found out Nanny has cancer. She had it before.'

'She had it before?' Lorenz repeated sharply. 'You didn't tell us.'

'No. No, I didn't. Because they caught it straight away, and it was fine, so I didn't think I needed to tell you.'

The kids absorbed this in silence.

'But now she's got it again. It's come back, and it's a bit worse.'

Tate was first with questions. 'So how is she? Is she going to be like Mummy?'

Tia was next. 'Is it bad? Is she going to come out? When's she coming out?'

'What type of cancer is it?' Lorenz asked quietly.

Tate began to babble. 'So they've got it under control? Or not? It's going to get like Mummy's one, isn't it? Is she going to die? She's going to die, isn't she?'

'I don't know,' I told them. 'She could make a full recovery and come home. Or she might have to stay in hospital for ever. Or she might die. We don't yet know which it will be.'

'So she could die, then?' Tate persisted.

'Yes, she could die.'

At the hospital Tia chatted away to Mum and played on her phone as if everything were perfectly normal. I didn't know if this was her way of coping, or if she was still too young to absorb the gravity of my news. Lorenz, as ever, was calm and quietly thoughtful, while Tate bombarded me with questions. 'What does that machine do? What do those flashing lights mean? What did that doctor just say to you? Is everything all right?'

That was two weeks ago. Since then all three have been more openly emotional than they ever are about their mum. There have been tears, and cuddles, and Tate has been sleeping in my bed again. Sometimes I wonder whether some of their tears are really for their mum, but easier to weep under the guise of grief for their grandmother. Or maybe my mother has given my children a second chance too, and, just like me, they're taking it. Perhaps we've all learned from my mistakes.

When my children were born, I thought I would always know how to be a good father. But if I've learned anything in the last thirty months, it's that raising a family is nothing like being a footballer. In real life there are no rules to guarantee fair play, and no referee to appeal to when Fate keeps fouling you. On the football pitch you can expect all your training and planning and discipline to pay off, that the team who works hardest will ultimately win. It seemed only logical to assume the same would apply to the rest of my life.

The last thirty months have forced me to see that my delusions of control were a fantasy. All of us are at the mercy of Fate, no matter how hard we work, and nobody has all the answers. There is no such thing as a perfect parent, and fatherhood is not all about winning.

The other day I was driving Tate home from football practice. We were chatting about his performance, and analysing tactics, when without warning he turned and raised his head to look straight at me.

'Dad. Who invented cancer? Why does it exist?'

For a moment I was floored. And then, quite suddenly, I saw. What Tate needed from me wasn't some clever pretence that I knew the answer. Why cancer had stolen away the two women my children love most is a mystery I will never solve. The unknowability of life is the only truth I can give them.

I glanced across at Tate and took his hand. 'I don't know, son. I just don't know.'

AFTERWORD

I COULD NEVER have guessed that a book about the death of my wife would end with the passing of my mum as well. In scarcely more than two years, my children and I have lost the two women we loved most in the world. As I write those words, I can still barely believe they are true. Our world will never be the same again.

I had planned to spend the summer holiday with the kids in Portugal, but before school broke up we already knew that was never going to happen. Mum was fading fast, and we had been in Portugal for less than a week when it became clear that time was running out.

I used to think I knew all about flying back to London in subdued spirits. I'd travelled home from enough foreign defeats to be familiar with the unique bleakness of a football team silenced by shame and dread. I knew how it felt to wish the plane would never land. What I didn't know, and would never have guessed, was that worse things can be waiting for you on the ground than tabloid reporters' taunts. When your journey's final destination is your mother's

247

deathbed, you'd give anything to be flying home from World Cup disgrace, knocked out by part-timers from an obscure principality.

Just as we were about to board the flight home from Portugal, I was seized by a sudden impulse to turn around, flee the airport and keep running as far as I could. Flying home to attend my mum's death seemed so surreal that it felt as if it would make me somehow complicit in it. By the same wild illogic, if I refused to go, I could somehow prevent it. But by then I knew the havoc grief can play with one's mind, and was not falling for its tricks.

Two days later I knew we were saying our final goodbye, when my brothers and sister, mum's husband Peter and I all gathered together around her hospital bed. I knew our love couldn't save her, and before our eyes on 13 July 2017, she passed away.

My wife and my mother were the twin pillars of my life, supporting everything most dear to me. When Rebecca died, were it not for my mum I don't know how I would have survived. Even in the depths of grief, I still had someone who knew me better than I knew myself, and loved me unconditionally. My children might have been motherless, but for as long as they had my mum they would always be mothered.

And now she is gone. Just at the very point when I had started to hope for happier times, and dared to think we were finding our feet, my family has been plunged back into the turmoil of loss all over again. The hole left in our lives by these two deaths feels like a gaping wound, and although I've learned enough about grief by now to know the bleeding will ease, and in time begin to heal, I also know that the hole can never be filled. Rebecca and my mother were and are irreplaceable.

How we will make peace with the enormity of our loss, I don't yet know. I do, though, wish more support could be offered to the newly bereaved. Every day, in every hospital, families like mine are watching someone they love die, and leave reeling and undone by grief. I know it's the job of hospitals to take care of the living, but when a patient dies, the loved ones left behind need care too. The medical consequences of grief can be very grave. Statistically, the bereaved become more at risk of all sorts of ailments, from insomnia to cancer, and whatever it would cost the NHS to radically upgrade its bereavement support services, I bet even more would be saved by preventing grief-related illness.

I do know that I'm one of the lucky ones. That's a funny thing to say after losing my wife and my mum, and I'm not trying to pretend I wake up each day feeling like a lucky guy. But I do feel incredibly fortunate to have met so many people who really understand grief, and have been able to help. Above all, I feel blessed by the love and support of those closest to me, who have stood by me and my children and taught us the true meaning of loyalty. I've never been a big one for nature, but I think I now get what people mean when they talk about life being like the seasons. From the death and decay of autumn and winter, new spring shoots grow, and something a bit like that has happened to my relationship with my dad.

Tragedy has brought me and my dad closer than I think either of us could ever have imagined. Ever since Rebecca died, he has been a rock for me and my kids – a constant presence in the house, solid and soothing, quietly seeing to the children's needs without fuss or any need for thanks. He didn't have the easiest start in life, but his determination to become a more loving and open father is a constant source of inspiration to me. He was always my hero, but never more so than now he has become the keystone of my family.

Before Rebecca died, our friendship with Jamie and Lisa was already so solid that I would probably have said it wasn't possible to get any closer. I was wrong. They have busy lives, three young kids of their own, and every reason to run out of patience for my three a.m. distress phone calls. And yet they've listened to me ramble incoherently until dawn, night after night, and every day they show my children as much love as they have for their own.

One of the worst things about widowhood is the shock of having no one to consult. In a marriage, collaboration becomes second nature, so to find yourself suddenly in sole executive charge of all decisions is terrifying. For someone like me, who finds trusting anyone so hard, the sudden isolation practically paralysed me with panic that I might, left to my own devices, make a disastrously unwise decision. But Jamie and Lisa became my sounding boards, dispensing wise and honest advice, even when it isn't what I want to hear – or not what they want to say.

Earlier this year, to my total surprise, I met someone and at first I wasn't sure I should let free my feelings. In an emotionally vulnerable state, one's judgement can be all over the place. I wanted to get to know this beautiful young woman better, and, as I have done on occasions, turned to Lisa for advice.

Of all the things Lisa has done for me, this may have been the hardest. Rebecca had been her best friend. It's a measure of Lisa's love that she put aside her own feelings, offered her friendship to this new stranger and gave the relationship her wholehearted encouragement. For that I will be forever in her debt.

If my mother's death was the last way I expected to end this book when I began, a new relationship would have struck me as barely any less unlikely. It has taken her by surprise, too, a widowed father of three not having figured on her radar as ideal match material. It takes courage and heart to take on a broken, traumatised family, and this is still early days for us. Neither of us underestimates the challenges that lie ahead.

All I know is that this book ends with my children and me beginning a new chapter. I've fallen for someone who is great for me but, importantly, great with my children too. We have someone new in our lives – and that alone feels like a miracle. My children seem so much happier with her around and I am getting more out of them through her.

To anyone reading this who has suffered loss and heartbreak, or who has already been in touch to offer support and share their own experiences with me, I hope it helps you to turn a page, too, and soon begin a new chapter of your own.

LETTERS OF SUPPORT

Rio,

Thank you for showing that as a man it isn't shameful to show or share your feelings and emotions. When my daughter was two she was diagnosed with liver and lung cancer. I spent almost three years battling inside to hold things together during her long treatment phase. I still struggle with my feelings and demons inside. I sat watching your documentary tonight and I broke down in front of my wife for the first time and let my worries, scares and everything I have bottled up for so long out. — David

Dear Rio,

Football is great, but relating how you see things in life is more important. I believe you will blow the lid on every subject that we the public do not know how to deal with. — Peter

Dear Rio,

I have never watched something before and felt like the need to contact a celebrity afterwards, but I did after watching your BBC documentary.

I think that your kids are going to be just fine, because you are willing to do whatever it takes to help them, whether you feel ready or not. And that takes an amazing amount of bravery and strength.

Unfortunately, my uncle (Dad's brother) didn't have that strength. My aunty died aged forty-two of breast cancer in 2009, leaving her three children, one girl and two boys, like your kids. My uncle really didn't cope with her death, neither of them accepted her prognosis and they didn't accept the counsellor's advice to talk to the kids before her death. Denying things just makes it worse. Unfortunately, denial is a big trait in my family.

In 2013 my uncle died from alcohol-related abuse. So well done for putting the drink down, we all need one now and then, but in our culture it's something that can be turned to too easily as a quick fix. And where does it leave the kids?

No one in my family – immediate and extended – talks about feelings or emotions. After watching you talk to the therapists and seeing what help is out there, you have inspired me to get everyone together, to have a type of collective memorial and share all our memories of everyone. Right after watching your programme I started a memory tin. So thank you. Your bravery and honesty in making that programme will help countless families, I'm sure. — Samantha

Dear Rio,
I watched your 'Being Mum and Dad' on iPlayer last night. Thank you for your openness and honesty – what an amazing thing that you've done for many thousands/millions of viewers.

You have helped me to appreciate my husband and my life just a little bit more. — Zara

Hi Rio,
I lost my son in September 2016, he was eleven days old. A healthy baby that came home and suddenly fell ill. I wanted to send a message to Rio to say thank you so much for his documentary. It made me realise how my husband felt with his grieving, it helped my husband talk to me about his son and express to me [that] the way Rio was feeling was exactly the same way he was feeling and still feeling. I think it was a fantastic documentary, it's going to help so many grieving fathers, husbands, brothers, etc., get through bereavement. Men do not express their feelings as much as women do, so I think it was very brave of Rio to do that. — Regena

Dear Rio,
I felt completely emotional and compelled to write having watched the documentary. I am a forty-two-year-old woman who lost my precious mum to cancer in 1983, at the age of eight. My sister was aged twelve and my mum was thirty-five. My dad struggled to give me the emotional support I needed. He was old school and very much a man's man, so didn't show emotion.
Unfortunately, nobody within the family could come to terms with what happened. Everybody was trapped within their own grief. Which in turn meant my mother was never spoken about. Thirty-four years on, I have no memories of my mother. I have locked them away somewhere in my mind as it is too painful to deal with.

I feel that if my mother's memory was kept alive then maybe I would have coped a lot better throughout my life. It is so important that you do your best to ensure your kids don't ever lose their memories of their mum, Rio. I can't stress enough how important this is. Coming from someone who knows. — Lisa

Hi Rio,

I've just watched your documentary and think you are incredibly brave for making it so soon after losing your wife. I lost my sister aged thirty-two to breast cancer five years ago and I really related to you when you said you have been keeping yourself busy in order to cope as that is exactly what I chose to do for about two years after she passed away.

I didn't get counselling and looking back now I wish I had – I did get on a waiting list but when I got the chance to go for it six months later I chose not to, and after watching your programme I see it could have helped me and may have channelled some guilt and anger that I felt. I'm sure making the documentary has helped you and many others – I know it touched my brother-in-law after he watched it and I hope that it helps him to finally seek counselling as he has struggled coping with her death. — Vicky

Hi Rio,

Firstly I want to say how much respect I have for you, for opening up and filming your documentary. I have only just watched it today because I knew I needed to be prepared for the upset.

I lost my dad in 2008, when I was just fifteen years old. At first everyone was around and fussed about me, everyone wanted to go for meals, go shopping. I was never left alone. I didn't know when I was to be alone how hard those moments were going to be.

I got through my last year of school and passed all my GCSEs, but no teacher ever talked about my dad with me and never really did anyone else. I never went to no groups to open up. I always thought my mum would be too upset if I talked to her about him so I never really opened up, and because of this I really suffered, I developed anxiety and was very depressed, sometimes I would get so angry and other times I would blame myself.

It took about four years until me and my mum would actually talk about him, about memories and about what happened. She told me that he didn't want me to know he actually had cancer, he didn't want me in the hospital room because he didn't want to let me down, he wanted me to think of him as strong.

I think that if I could have had the chance to open up and talk about my dad earlier and grieved, I wouldn't have had such dark times. Your programme has reminded me that it is OK to talk and ask questions, even eight years on you still need to talk. Thank you very much. — Sally

Hi Rio,

I just watched your documentary – wow, what a hard watch! I cried all the way through. I lost my mum eleven years ago, when I was just nine. Your documentary, your words really touched me – I can relate to everything you said. I just wanted to say thank you for doing this – I have no doubt that it will help hundreds of bereaved parents and children across the country. Your documentary made me realise that although it's been eleven years, I never truly got over my mum's passing. I've never spoken to anyone about it and we never truly dealt with it as a family – we all just tried to move on and became busy with school, careers, uni, etc., (I'm a medical student now!). I'm still grieving, all these years later. You've inspired me to try and go to a bereavement counselling service with my siblings to talk about our mum and try and deal with our grief. I wish the best for both you and your family – I'm sure your wife would be very proud of you all. — Afra

Dear Rio,

I was so touched by the grace and love in which you have dealt with your loss. As someone who has recently lost a loved one I can understand your pain. As a mental health professional I want to thank you and your friends for sharing your stories of loss. Nothing is more powerful than hearing these stories and raising awareness of these issues. I truly hope you will all find peace and happiness in the future.

Thank you so much for sharing your story. You probably have no idea how much it will help other men going through similar experiences. There's a lot of research on the reluctance of males to seek help for emotional problems. — Helen

WHERE TO FIND HELP

The following groups offer help to adults:

BEREAVEMENTUK.CO.UK

This website operates an online support group with more than two thousand members.

LOSS OF A CHILD

Facebook group for bereaved parents
Moderators: Sue Hughes and Carolyn Brice, info@tcf.org.uk

PARENTS BEREAVED BY SUICIDE

Facebook group
Moderator: Marie Best, mariebest76@gmail.com

PARENTS BEREAVED BY ADDICTION

Facebook group
Moderator: Susan Brooks, susanc15@live.co.uk

BEREAVED DADS
Facebook group
Moderator: Paul Cooke and John Robertson, info@tcf.org.uk

Two informal Facebook groups have been created to organise social meet-ups with other bereaved parents. All are welcome to join:

COMPASSIONATE PALS – SOUTH OF ENGLAND
contact: info@tcf.org.uk

COMPASSIONATE PALS – NORTH OF ENGLAND & SCOTLAND
contact: info@tcf.org.uk

Here are some organisations that help young people and children:

Hope Again – Cruse Bereavement Care's website for young people. It has personal stories, videos, blogs, advice, and encourages interaction. It's aimed at teens. (Cruse is a national charity that provides support, advice and information to children, young people and adults when someone close to them dies.) hopeagain.org.uk

Winston's Wish – the first child bereavement charity set up in the UK, they run drop-ins across the country, a range of specialist support, support in schools, and have great lists of resources, including books, activities, etc. winstonswish.org.uk

CHUMS – what started as a child bereavement charity is now a nationwide mental health and emotional wellbeing service for children and young people. You can refer your child to them for specialist counselling for grief and trauma, and they have specialists to help children and young people who may have lost a parent in a sudden and traumatic manner. chums.uk.com

Child Bereavement UK – work with families losing a child as well as bereaved kids. Helpline number: 0800 028 8840. They run support services across the UK. childbereavementuk.org

Childline – general confidential support hotline for kids who might be facing problems and want to talk about it with someone. On their website they offer a bunch of resources to do with losing a parent and their phone operators are trained to talk with bereaved kids. Hotline number: 0800 1111. childline.org.uk

Childhood Bereavement Network – a hub for charities, therapists and counsellors who run support services for bereaved kids. A great starting place for finding out about different kinds of support, and where and how to access them. childhoodbereavementnetwork.org.uk

Jigsaw (South East) – a charity based in Surrey that offers support groups to bereaved children and young people in the area who have lost a significant family member. They have also partnered with Macmillan to offer support to children and young people who have family members suffering from terminal illnesses. jigsawsoutheast.org.uk

ACKNOWLEDGEMENTS

LIKE MOST ACHIEVEMENTS in my life, this book has been a team effort, and I could not have asked for a better squad. The first person I want to thank is Jamie Moralee, my agent and friend, for standing by my side through the best and worst of times, and building a post-football career for me that any player in the world would be proud of. Without Jamie, *Thinking Out Loud* would not even exist. When I was newly widowed, and barely knew my own mind, it was Jamie who suggested the idea of a film about me learning to grieve, and from that seed this book grew. His wife Lisa was one of Rebecca's closest friends, and Lisa's love for my late wife has shone on since her death, through her boundless support and kindness to me and my children. They have been true friends to us, and we will be forever in their debt.

As soon as I decided to write the book, I knew I wanted Decca Aitkenhead to help me. Her own extraordinary, brave story *All at Sea* about the death of her partner leaving her with two young sons was a real inspiration to me. I knew she would understand so much. I can't thank her enough for her intensive time, skills – and friendship – in helping me to find the words and make this book the best it could be.

Grant Best, my creative director and who produced the documentary *Being Mum and Dad*, has been a constant source of wise counsel, and his contribution to this book has been invaluable. Whenever I've had doubts or felt uncertain, I have been able to rely on his judgement, and to work so closely with someone whose instincts I can always trust means the world to me. I've also been blessed to have a perceptive and diligent reader while writing this book, and want to thank Justin Rigby, my publicist, for being my second pair of eyes, as well as all the great team at New Era for their support.

My editors at Hodder, Rowena Webb and Hannah Black, are entirely to thank for making this whole process more painless than I could ever have imagined. Their empathy, tact and sensitivity have made all the difference in the world. They believed in this book, and knew what it could be, long before even I did, and for their faith and guidance I am profoundly grateful. My thanks too to Lucy Hale, Louise Swannell, Caitriona Horne, Ian Wong and everyone at Hodder for helping me to get this book into as many hands as possible.

The book was inspired by the TV documentary I made about learning to grieve, and I want to thank everyone at the BBC who worked on the film. It was an intensely personal and highly emotional project, and I am grateful beyond words to them for helping to create a film that has meant so much to so many people. I owe a huge debt of gratitude to the people I met while filming – Ben Brooks-Dutton and his widowers' group, Darren Clarke, and everyone at Jigsaw South East and Child Bereavement UK, in particular Mark and Emily.

I didn't know it at the time, but the documentary would mark a turning point in my life, and set me on the long path towards recovery from grief. It literally changed my life.

I could not have written this without the contributions of close family and friends, whose memories have been a crucial part of the story. Even when desperately ill, my mum still devoted herself to helping to the very end, with the same selfless love she showed me from the day I was born. My dad remarked recently that he couldn't think of a single difference between him and me, but in the course of writing this book I've discovered one big one: he has a way, way better memory than mine! His thoughtful recollections of our family history have helped me understand much about my background and myself, and are another measure of the man and father he is to me. A special mention too to my brother and sisters – at times just being there was all that I needed. And I want to thank Rebecca's family, especially her parents, Steven and Lesley, for sharing their memories of her childhood. I learnt a lot about Rebecca through writing the book, and will always treasure every precious new detail they shared. Their loss goes beyond words, and I am eternally grateful to them for all their support. Sandra has been with my family through unimaginable heartbreak, and her input was yet another gift to us for which we are forever thankful. Another wonderful friend to the family is Lisa Dixon and I thank her too for everything she does to support us. The friend I made in childhood Gavin Rose is a friend forever – thank you for always being there.

My PA, Tucker Davey, has fielded endless queries and requests with her unfailing patience and good nature. I also want to thank April Willis for meticulously transcribing all the hours and hours of taped conversation, and Matilda Munro for her tireless research into studies of bereavement and grief.

Lastly, I want to thank my three beautiful children. They are my world, my pride and joy, and I simply could not have gone on without them. One day, when they read this book, I hope they take comfort and strength from seeing in black and white just how deeply their mum loved them.

PICTURE ACKNOWLEDGEMENTS

Most of the photographs are from the family collection.

Additional sources: © Back Page Images/REX/Shutterstock, page 70.
© Colorsport/REX/Shutterstock, page 80.

INDEX

Page numbers in **bold** refer to photographs.

An invitation from the publisher

Join us at www.hodder.co.uk, or follow us
on Twitter @hodderbooks to be a part of
our community of people who love the very
best in books and reading.

Whether you want to discover more about a book
or an author, watch trailers and interviews, have the
chance to win early limited editions, or simply browse
our expert readers' selection of the very best books,
we think you'll find what you're looking for.

And if you don't, that's the place to tell us what's missing.

We love what we do, and we'd love you to be a part of it.

www.hodder.co.uk

@hodderbooks

HodderBooks

HodderBooks